My Search for Catherine Anne

Liz + Dave.

For your help
and support — Please
keep in touch;

Barrie.

My Search for Catherine Anne

One Man's Story of an Adoption Reunion

Barrie A. Clark

James Lorimer & Company, Publishers
Toronto, 1989

Front cover photos: Jim Morrison and Ken Fleet

Canadian Cataloguing in Publication Data

Clark, Barrie A.
  My Search for Catherine Anne

Bibliography: p. 153
ISBN 1-55028-205-0 (bound) ISBN 1-55028-203-4 (pbk.)

1. Clark, Barrie A.. 2. Adoptees - Canada -
Identification. 3. Fathers - Canada - Biography.
I. Title.

HV874.82.C42A3 1989   362.7'34'0971   C89-093553-X

James Lorimer & Company Limited
Egerton Ryerson Memorial Building
35 Britain Street
Toronto, Ontario
M5A 1R7

Printed and bound in Canada

6 5 4 3 2 1 # 89 90 91 92 93 94

*To Inge,
for understanding*

Table of Contents

Introduction

The motivation to write this book came as a result of much pressure and encouragement from those many friends who shared my disappointments and frustrations during the search for my daughter. They wanted me to succeed in my efforts almost as much as I did myself. In the end, they convinced me to tell my story, if for no other reason, as an encouragement to others.

It was originally my intention to deal only with the search itself. However, as so often happens, the book took on a life of its own. Whether I had wanted to or not, I had become embroiled in an important social issue involving thousands of Canadians. It is my hope that by telling my story I may bring to public attention the plight of the adopted. I have tried to do this so that the story may inspire public discussion and debate about our well intentioned but misguided adoption laws.

To all my friends who encouraged me when I was low and suggested new ways I might renew my search, my thanks are best expressed in the joy they know I now share with my lovely daughter and her family.

No man could ask for more understanding and support than I received from my wife Inge. Both my search and this book would have been impossible without her.

My daughter Janet Fleet tells her own story as our two searches coincide. She has my very special thanks for joining me in this project. Her motivation also is to call attention to the urgent need for change in adoption law.

Carol is not the real name of my high school sweetheart and the mother of my daughter. She now lives a productive and happy life with her own family and I respect her privacy.

Barrie Clark
West Vancouver, BC
1989

1

There's Something I Want To Tell You

The plane had begun its descent as Calgary came into view, frozen in the deep grip of winter. The grey white landscape looked uninviting to a west coaster, used as I am to the greens and blues of the Pacific. I am a proud Canadian, but the prairies have always seemed like another country to me. The landscape is so flat and vast. I know that's why the locals love it but to me it is dull and cold compared to the mountains, inlets and roaring breakers of the coast.

This was a weekend business trip with an important meeting scheduled for Sunday morning. Tonight, however, I had something very personal planned. I was rather apprehensive about it, not being absolutely sure about either my motivation or the outcome. The telephone call I intended to make as soon as I reached my hotel was the result of a long series of events that had begun over thirty years before. I hoped to speak to an old girlfriend from my high school years.

I had never tried to locate Carol until soon after attending a class reunion. It was the thirtieth reunion of my graduating class from our high school. It was both a happy and sad occasion for me, as most such reunions probably are for those in attendance. I was happy to see some of my old schoolmates but sad there was so little now in common between us. While I was dancing with May, one of the girls who had been a mutual friend of Carol's and mine, I learned where she now lived.

After the dance, I told my wife Inge about what I had learned from May. "Now you must find out her address and write her," Inge said. "She was special to you and you must find out how she is." This proved to be easier than I had expected, as a friend of mine was working for a television station in the same city as Carol lived in. I phoned him and asked if he would use his reporter's skills and find Carol's address for me, as well as anything else he could discover about her. He succeeded in doing this and I wrote Carol a short letter saying I had met May at the school reunion and that she had mentioned where she was living.

In her reply, Carol seemed genuinely happy to hear from me after all the years. She gave me a brief description of what had happened to her since we had last met and said she would like to meet me if I was ever in town. I left it at that and another eight months passed before an urgent business meeting required me to fly east. Now I was circling over her city. It did not look inviting. I had left Vancouver in spring-like weather and I did not welcome the sudden blast of cold as the aircraft door opened.

Inge had made me promise to call, which was rather puzzling to those who learned later how that telephone call was to change our lives. "Remember to call Carol as soon as you arrive," she said. "Take her out for a nice dinner and have a good talk. It will be fun."

I did call her as soon as I had checked in to my hotel and she agreed to join me for dinner that evening. I went down to the lobby to seek advice about a good restaurant. The clerk at the front desk gave me long face saying, "You'll be lucky to get a reservation. Everything is pretty well booked."

With the encouragement of a large tip, the clerk obtained a table for us at one of the city's better restaurants. I set off in a taxi, looking forward to an enjoyable evening, sharing old memories and catching up on what Carol had been doing for the past thirty years. As the cab left the hotel, I realized why I had experienced such difficulty in making a dinner reservation — it was Feb. 14, 1981, Saint Valentine's Day.

There was only a moment's embarrassment when Carol met me at the door. We laughed about time's effect, and particularly how grey my hair had become. I met her youngest daughter, now a university student and just about the exact age Carol had been when I had last seen her. Then, with the taxi waiting outside, we left for dinner.

We reminisced about our days together in the picturesque town we had both grown up in and loved so much, perched as it was on the edge of a crystal-clear lake in the interior of British Columbia. We agreed that our own children were not as fortunate as we had been in living in such idyllic surroundings as young people. Over dinner it took hardly any time at all to fill in the intervening years, which had treated us both rather kindly. Carol had completed her musical studies, eventually marrying a fellow student. She went with him to England where he was to continue his studies. There they began their family, which soon included a son and two daughters.

Returning to Canada, they settled into the musical life of this bustling city, but their marriage did not survive. Carol undertook further education to equip her to raise her three children on her own. This she had done successfully, building her independence and earning a respected place in her community.

Carol suggested that we leave the restaurant and return to her home for coffee. She added, "There's something I want to tell you." In the taxi I wondered what she meant, but it had to wait as she chatted away about other things. She told me of the musical achievements of her children and asked about members of my family, particularly my younger sister who, years before, used to accompany us on many of our skating excursions.

Back at the house, Carol put on the coffee and opened a bottle of Grand Marnier that she had bought with earnings from playing the organ at a wedding earlier in the day. We settled down to an easy talk about old friends and what they were doing now. I finally reminded her of her statement in the restaurant that she wanted to tell me something. She just looked at me for several seconds as if she wasn't sure she wanted to continue our talk at all. Then her eyes filled with tears and she dropped her gaze, staring into her lap.

I put an arm around her shoulder and asked, "Carol, what's the matter? Have I said something to upset you?"

She shook her head, paused again for several seconds and then, almost in a whisper, said, "When you left Toronto, I didn't know it at the time, but I was pregnant."

I was stunned. I felt chilled, as if the cold I had been fighting all day had suddenly taken hold. "When did you find out?" I stammered.

"A little over two months after you left," she replied.

"What did you do? Why didn't you tell me?"

Very slowly and quietly, amidst a lot of tears, the story came out. After I had left Toronto, she had gone to the doctor and discovered she was pregnant. She spent days worrying about what to do. Even if abortion had been readily available at that time, it was out of the question for her. She would have the baby. How she could continue her studies without everyone recognizing her secret was a real problem — she would need help and she would have to tell her parents.

I still shudder at the thought. I had liked her parents well enough but I had always been afraid of her father. He acknowledged my presence around the house but seldom spoke to me, and I don't believe I ever saw him smile. Carol's mother, in contrast, was always nice to me. She sang with Carol and me in the church choir and had known me for many years. The only concern she had ever expressed to me was the late hours I shared with her daughter, particularly since we both usually had classes the next day.

After discussing the problem with her parents, Carol decided she would remain in Toronto. The university term would end before her pregnancy became too noticeable and the baby would be born sometime in early October, just after the new term began. She could create an excuse for her absence from the first few weeks of classes. No one outside the immediate family would learn the truth. My parents would remain ignorant. No one in our town would ever know a thing about it. Most important of all, Carol would give up the baby for adoption, never revealing to anyone but her parents that I was the father.

Suddenly, my mind went back to our final meeting on the sidewalk outside our hometown church. I now realized that she must have been about four months pregnant then. Carol told me she had almost broken down and revealed her secret to me. Had she done so, I know I would have wanted to marry her immediately, but we were very young. Carol's education was at stake and I had demonstrated my inability to hold a job. The decision was made. The baby would be given up for adoption and I would never know.

When the university term finished, Carol moved to the Presbyterian Home for Unwed Mothers in Toronto. The staff made everything as pleasant as possible for her, even providing a piano for her use. The summer passed somehow. She was on her own, away from family, and nauseous with morning sickness. Meanwhile, blissfully unaware, I was making preparations for entering the ministry and attending university in Vancouver.

Carol gave birth to a healthy baby girl. She signed the adoption consent papers, the father's identity not disclosed. Carol saw her baby before she left the hospital and noted a tiny birthmark on one ear. She used her mother's right to name her child. The adoption papers showed the given names — Catherine Anne. Those were the names of Carol's aunt and my young sister.

Now, sitting in Carol's living room, we were both distraught and exhausted. The coffee was untouched on the table before us. Questions raced through my mind. "What would have happened if I'd known?" "If we had married, how would our lives have turned out?" "Would we have been happy?" We each now had three children. They would not have been born if we'd married. In my heart I knew most of the answers — Carol and her parents had been right. We were too young. It simply wouldn't have worked. Nonetheless, I felt a surge of anger over not being told the truth and having been denied any say in the decision about what happened to my daughter.

Part of my mind denied what Carol had told me. This could not be happening to me. I thought back to our last day together — I remembered my cheap rented room. I had given the very suspicious landlord some crazy story about a relative having to wait for a bus. He had eventually agreed to let me bring Carol to my room. Inside, I had taken the single wooden chair and jammed it up under the doorknob. We wanted to be alone in our sadness at parting.

I counted the months — yes, this baby Carol was telling me about, this tiny girl she had named Catherine Anne, was my daughter.

"Why have you told me now?" I asked.

"I'd thought of telling you many times," she said "but I didn't know what happened to you or where you were. I'd heard from someone you were in radio but that was all. It wasn't until we were at dinner together tonight that I knew I wanted you to know."

"It's more than that," I suggested. "Do you want me to try and find her?"

"No, I don't want to interfere in her life," Carol responded quickly.

"Maybe I could find her without her ever knowing."

It was well past midnight. I could see Carol's self-control stretching to the breaking point and I too was emotionally drained. I suggested that I return to my hotel, we both try to get some sleep, and I would call her in the morning.

Back in my hotel room, I tried to fall asleep but it was impossible. I was exhausted but my mind wouldn't stop buzzing. Somewhere out there I had a thirty-year-old daughter. Where was she? What was she doing? Suddenly, the awful thought struck that she could be dead. Maybe she had been killed in a traffic accident when she was just a teenager. Pushing that thought from my mind, I wondered if she knew she was adopted. Did she ever wonder about her real mother? Did she ever think of me?

Eventually, I did fall asleep but only for an hour or so. I awoke with a monstrous headache and a raging fever. My business meeting was in the hotel in about an hour. I ordered breakfast and phoned Carol, telling her I had to see her again. There was much more I wanted to know and we had not fully discussed what exactly I was to do with the startling information she had revealed to me. I agreed to cut short my meeting in order to give us an hour before my flight home.

The business meeting was a blur. By this time it was evident I was suffering from a bad cold and I could hardly concentrate on the matters under discussion. I hoped the others in attendance blamed my incoherence on my cold. I made up some story about receiving news overnight which forced me to attend another meeting later in the morning — actually that excuse was not far off the mark.

I rushed back to my room, packed my bag and dashed outside where Carol was waiting in her car. She admitted to being as weary as I was, sleep having escaped her as well. We were much calmer and not nearly as emotional as we discussed again many of the things we had talked about the previous evening. I suggested again that one of the principal reasons she had revealed her long-kept secret to me was that I might be able to determine whether or not

Catherine Anne was alive and well. Carol agreed and I took notes of everything she could remember of what had happened in the hospital and during the adoption proceedings.

There was not much to go on. The baby was born on Oct. 7, 1952, in Toronto's Women's College Hospital. From there she was taken home by her adopting parents. The Presbyterian Home for Unwed Mothers must have arranged the adoption. The only other thing Carol remembered was that she had written a detailed letter about our family backgrounds, without revealing identities, and had given it to the social workers. In that letter, she had made a strong plea for her daughter to have a musical education. That was the only information I had.

Promising to keep in close contact, I left for the airport.

I sat in the waiting room after checking in for my flight. There I experienced for the first, but not the last time, an eerie feeling. My daughter might be sitting right there in the room with me. I glanced around at all the women who might be the right age, trying to recognize a family resemblance to either Carol or me. As silly as it now seems, I imagined that at least two of the women sitting there with me might be her.

On the plane flying back to Vancouver, I felt the same strange sensation. What if my daughter was on this very plane with me? I would not even know her. I looked at all the female passengers around me, as well as the flight attendants. This phenomenon would repeat itself several times on later occasions and always left me emotionally upset. I realize now that it arose from a deep longing to discover what had happened to the daughter I had never known. This was combined with a feeling of hopelessness over what seemed to be the insurmountable difficulties confronting me in any search that I might undertake. The feeling would occur without warning in a shopping mall, a bank lineup, even when I was taking my daily walk.

Now, on the way home, my mind traced the unexpected events of the weekend. For a moment, I toyed again with the idea that Carol was not being truthful with me. There had to be some other explanation — I could not possibly be the father of her child; this sort of thing happened only to other people. Immediately, I was ashamed of the thought. There was no reason for her to lie and, besides, the timing and circumstances were right. I was the father of a grown daughter, almost thirty years old.

The trip went quickly — before I knew it I was back in the Vancouver airport. After collecting my suitcase, I walked to my car and began the drive through the city to my home. In the traffic, each mile along the way brought with it another question. How would Inge react to my news? She certainly had not expected anything like this when she encouraged me to make contact again with Carol. What would my sons' reaction be when they learned they had a sister? How would this news effect my mother and the other members of my family? What would my friends say? This was not like some of the other surprises I had sprung on them over the years. This was admitting to a relationship with Carol that had been far more than singing in the choir together.

Even more important, there was a little girl out there; no, not little any more, she was now almost thirty. I had fathered her but deserted her, leaving her to be raised by some people I did not even know. I suddenly knew how Carol had felt all these years, telling no one of her sadness, her regrets, her longing. It did not matter that I had not known about Catherine Anne before last evening. I still felt that I had betrayed her.

I realized that this feeling was no more than self-pity. My cold had taken a firm hold on me and I was very tired. I wanted to get home as soon as possible. I desperately needed to talk to Inge. Since boarding the plane, I had wondered how I was going to break this news to her. It never entered my mind that she would be angry or hurt by what I had to tell her, but still I was apprehensive. This was not the sort of news a wife expected to hear when her husband returned from a business trip.

As soon as I walked into the house, Inge knew something very important was bothering me. "Are you alright?" she asked.

"Yes," I replied, "but I really have to talk to you."

Inge looked at me closely. "You sit down. I'll pour us both a drink and you can tell me all about it."

She knew instinctively that something had happened between Carol and me. "Did you have dinner with Carol?" she asked.

There was no way I could think of to prepare her, so I just blurted out, "I've got a daughter. When I left Carol in Toronto back in 1952, she was pregnant. She had the baby and gave her up for adoption."

Slowly, with Inge's patient help, I managed to put the events in some kind of order. She listened quietly as I repeated to her everything Carol had told me. By the time I had finished, I was again emotionally exhausted.

Inge stated simply, "Well, we're just going to have to find her."

Much later, Inge told me that she really was very happy with the news that I had a daughter. She had wanted to give me one but that being impossible, this was the next best thing. She was determined to help me in every way to find her.

In the days and weeks ahead, many women told me they did not know what they would have done if their husbands had come home with a confession such as mine. Most marvelled at Inge's calm reaction. Much to my amazement, some admitted that their marriage might not have survived such a turn of events. Few suggested that they would have followed Inge's example by joining in the search for their husband's daughter.

2

Two Women In My Life

The story of how I met Inge resembles a fairy tale. My first marriage had ended and I was living in a small apartment in Vancouver's west end, which I had chosen for the sweeping view of the ocean. It had remained unappreciated for six months as I resisted the break and separation from my three growing sons, but finally I moved in and tried to sort out my life. It was a new bachelorhood which I found lonely and unsatisfying.

One afternoon, I was walking from the radio station where I worked to my apartment when I met an old and dear friend, the local public relations officer for Canadian Pacific Airlines. Jim knew of my situation and suggested that what I needed was a break from work and my personal worries. His airline had just inaugurated a new flight to Israel and he proposed that I take my holidays and fly the new route. All he wanted me to do in exchange was to talk about my trip on my afternoon radio program when I returned.

I was in the practice of resisting such offers but this proposal was timely and attractive. Getting away would probably do me a lot of good. Besides, I was in the mood for a change of scenery. Jim suggested that I stop over for a few days in Amsterdam and he gave me the name of a woman at the city's tourist bureau.

"I'll telex her you are coming," he said. "She'll look after you and show you the city."

Before I knew it, I was flying "over the Pole" to Holland. It was late afternoon when I checked into the hotel Jim had booked for me. As I had promised, I phoned the tourist bureau and asked for the woman Jim had mentioned. Unknown to me, his telex had caused a minor panic in that office, since a visiting party of sixteen journalists from Yugoslavia and Czechoslovakia had already taxed their hostess service to the limit. They finally decided that there was nothing else to be done but attach me to this unlikely group.

I was beginning to look forward to a night on the town when the hotel desk called me to say that the party I expected was waiting in the lobby. I emerged from the elevator to be met by a very attractive woman who quickly shattered my expectations of a night of fun and entertainment by asking, "Where is your tape machine?"

"In my room," I replied.

"Well, you'd better go and get it," she instructed.

I found myself returning obediently to my room for my tape recorder, although I didn't have the slightest intention of turning it on — particularly for this bossy woman.

She bustled me out of the hotel and into her car, whereupon she explained that our evening would begin at an Indonesian restaurant. "You'll enjoy the group you're joining," she explained in her perfect English. "They're a group of radio journalists just like yourself." She neglected to mention their nationalities or the distinct chance that language difficulties might impede polite dinnertime conversation.

I was soon in some doubt whether we would ever reach our destination, as my hostess wove her way through the narrow, traffic-filled streets. We dodged across the bicycle lanes and tram lines, finally ending up in a treed square where I followed a pointed finger to what was obviously our destination. The only problem was finding a place to park — at least, I thought it was a problem. To my astonishment, my driver leapt the curb and landed us between a lamp standard, a stone wall and the car ahead, but on the sidewalk, if you please.

"Are you going to leave it here on the sidewalk?" I asked.

"Of course," she said brusquely to me, the inconvenient stranger who was not yet used to the Amsterdammer's skill at planting cars on sidewalks, walkways or anywhere else barely large enough to hold them.

Inside the restaurant, I met my fellow journalists. As I feared, language was a very big problem. I finally found a Norwegian writer and broadcaster who, at least, spoke a few words of English. My hostess had long since disappeared to the other end of the room, leaving me to face an Indonesian *rysttafel* or rice table. This was something I had never before experienced. No matter which dish I tried, it was extremely hot and contained dozens of large staring eyes, belonging to tiny fish that huddled amidst steaming rice. I settled for the excellent Dutch beer and was greatly relieved when the announcement came to leave for a candlelight cruise down the canals of the beautiful historic city.

The canals of Amsterdam are high on my list of romantic settings. Our glass-covered launch drifted along the narrow waterways, parting the shadows of eight-hundred-year-old buildings along the banks. I sipped chilled white wine and soaked in the beauty of it all, marvelling at the narrow clearance as we passed under the floodlit arched stone bridges. I had given up on my fellow travellers. They seemed absorbed in the challenge of downing the ample supply of wine. I had moved to the front of the boat and was chatting with the skipper when my hostess noted that I had strayed from the pack.

When she asked if the company bored me, I replied frankly that communication with my fellow journalists was impossible. "Anyway," I said, "this is too beautiful for boisterous conversation."

She seemed to appreciate how much the beauty of the canals had moved me. She said, "They don't need me here anymore. I will be getting off at the next bridge. Would you like to come with me?"

"Yes, please," I quickly replied, not knowing where we might end up next.

She led me along the canal and down a narrow cobblestone alley to my first brown pub. These tiny cosy establishments are found on virtually every Amsterdam street, if you know where to look. They get their name from the dark aged oak panelling that always seems to line their walls. This one was one of my guide's favorites and we tucked into a small booth beside a rather battered piano. Before it sat a plump, balding gentleman who clearly enjoyed the ambience of his tiny concert hall. Perhaps this was because of the ready supply of the product of the house, a rough Dutch brandy, which I soon observed he favoured.

The pianist obviously knew my partner as they exchanged kisses and hugs and he began playing songs he knew were her favorites. Relaxed, sipping brandy and strong coffee, I looked again at my hostess for the evening. I had not once touched the tape recorder she had insisted I bring along. There had been no one who spoke English to interview — even if I had wanted to, which I definitely had not. She did not seem to care and, like me, was thankful to be free of her pestering journalists. She asked about Jim, our mutual friend who had arranged the trip for me. Our conversation turned to personal matters.

Inge told me that she had been born in Indonesia, but moved to Holland after the war. As a stewardess for KLM, she had seen much of the world. She, like I, was divorced and had taken some considerable time to create a new life for herself. This she had eventually succeeded in doing and was now totally immersed in the promotion of a city she loved so very much. We laughed over Jim's telex and the panic it caused, and how awkward I felt with the evening's company.

Despite the thousands of miles between us, we had much in common. We loved music and peace and beautiful things like old houses, furniture and paintings. Over the next three days we saw a lot of each other. Something very special had happened between us. But it couldn't go on for long — I had a schedule to keep.

Israel was even more exciting than I expected. I soaked in the sights and smells of old Jerusalem and stood silently before the holy places of three great religions. I admired the planted forests and groves and marvelled at the vibrant enthusiasm of the young men and women of the kibbutzim. I climbed the Mount of Olives and wandered through the ruins of Capernaum. I ate "Peter's fish" by the Sea of Galilee. Returning to Jerusalem, I visited the Knesset and listened to instantaneous translation of the debates taking place in that day's parliamentary session. Close by, I shuddered in horror at the heartrending memorial to the Holocaust.

I wanted to do a story on the peace-keeping troops so I flew to Cyprus and sat in the stifling bars of Nicosia, listening to the stories of lonely Canadian soldiers. They described the boring hours in barbed-wire enclosures atop the crumbling ruins of centuries old cathedrals; the only glamour to their job was in the newspaper stories back home. I flew on to Athens.

My room in Athens was hot and noisy and showed barely a trace of its once graceful hospitality to visiting British dignitaries and genteel tourists. What *was* special was the bathtub — it was the largest I had ever seen. My lanky six feet four inches fitted easily and I wallowed in the white porcelain coolness. Then I spotted the telephone. I had never seen a telephone by a bath before. A sudden inspiration came to me. With the help of a patient hotel operator who was used to the sudden wishes of hotel guests, I was soon talking to Inge in Amsterdam. She agreed to meet my plane the next day, enabling us to spend a few more days together before I boarded my flight back home.

I returned to Europe four months later, this time to the island of Corfu and a rudimentary straw hut in a Club Med. Since our parting, Inge and I had corresponded and monopolized the long-distance lines. This meeting was to determine if there was any logic at all in our looking to a future together. Inge later told me that she was putting me to the test: if I could survive old army cots, straw mattresses, French arrogance and Greek food, did not clamour for ice in every drink and did not need a little strip of paper across the biffy seat telling me it had been sanitized for my protection, maybe there was hope for this North American after all. It was a sun-soaked setting with the straw huts scattered under the trees of an old olive grove.

It was a perfect place to talk. Inge was unafraid of the idea of moving to a new city and country but was dreadfully worried about my sons. How would they accept a stepmother from a foreign country, especially one who spoke with a funny accent? She didn't even cook the kind of meals they liked. And I understood her heartbreak at the thought of leaving her family and so many dear friends in Amsterdam.

We shared the stories of our past, of our broken marriages, of our loves and lovers. It was then I told Inge about Carol. She wanted to know everything about her. "She was your first real girlfriend. It's important to me," she said. After some persuasion, I went back almost thirty years in my memory.

Carol and I had begun "going steady" when I was in grade eleven. She was a year ahead of me and our paths seldom crossed at school. It was in the church choir that we met and shared a growing love of music. I walked her home after church and choir practice and joined a music appreciation group to spend another evening with our friends and our music. Carol was a far better musician than

I — I was content to sit as an encouraging member of the audience at the many music competitions where she gathered the laurels that eventually took her away to Toronto to study.

A mutual love of music brought us together as teenagers. It also isolated us from our schoolmates, to whom organized sports were far more important. Neither Carol nor I was very athletic, so we spent more and more time together or with our small circle of friends who practised piano or singing. Once, we filled the young romantic leads in the local operetta, which was hardly the musical highlight of the year but was successful enough to raise the funds needed for new choir gowns.

In winter, we rode our bikes to the hills behind the town and joined our friends clearing one of the small frozen lakes. We shovelled for hours and enjoyed every minute of it. A rest around the bonfire on shore quickly warmed tingling fingers, and after lacing on our skates, off we went, hand in hand, around the lake. The air was icy cold and the sky a clear deep blue. We were young, healthy and happy in our teenaged love.

Summer sunshine, with school closed, saw us lying on one of the secluded beaches along the lake, splashing and diving into the water when the burning sand became too hot. Or we would cycle into the hills and climb to a spot overlooking the lake and valley, private and safe from all eyes, particularly those of our parents. It was inevitable that we, like so many teenagers everywhere, discovered a physical love, known only to ourselves.

In the 1940s, our town was a perfect place to live. Thinking back now, I believe that after the ravages of the war, the men must have come back determined to make their community everything they had dreamed of during those long years overseas. It was an honest town. The people were good. Those of us who grew up there were privileged.

Of course, we were all big band fans, with Sinatra, Como, Stafford and Shore vying for our affection. The boys wore strides, the girls bobbysocks and saddle shoes. We practised the jitterbug for hours. I remember two graduation dances with Carol, hers a year before mine. We danced together in the ballroom of the community aquatic centre on the shores of the lake.

With the moon painting the calm water a brilliant orange and the weeping willows dipping their long tendrils into the sand, the surroundings could not have been more romantic. We took off our shoes and walked along the shore, listening to the sounds of the band echoing across the water. Back in the ballroom, we danced close in each other's arms to the soft sentimental ballads of the day.

Both Carol's parents and mine had expressed their concerns about the amount of time we spent together, particularly in the evenings. They had high ambitions for us and did not want us to do something foolish. In their eyes, we were far too serious — far too young to be making any plans for the future. They were thankful when it all came to an end. At least, they thought it had. Carol finished high school and left for Toronto where she moved into residence at the university.

For almost a year we exchanged letters. I was determined to keep our love alive by leaving home and travelling east to be near her again. When school ended, much to my parents concern, I announced my intention to follow Carol to Toronto, the hub of radio broadcasting. There I would impress local radio station owners with my deep voice. Our high school had a radio club which produced a weekly program of entertainment and school news on the local radio station. I had been a member for a couple of years when the owner offered me a summer job as an announcer. This had been my career ambition for some time and I worked every hour I could find in order to develop a professional announcing style.

In 1951, there were only two ways of crossing the country, by train or by road. I could not afford either the train or the bus so I packed my few belongings into my grandfather's old leather grip and set out to hitchhike. On the way, I met wonderful people, interested in what I was doing and where I was going. They would often buy me lunch in the little prairie restaurants. Once, a policeman gave me a ride to the end of his patrol area. I usually stayed in the local YMCA or visited the small town radio stations where the night announcer frequently let me bunk down with him.

It took me five days to reach Thunder Bay, where I had heard I might be able to sign on a grain boat to Toronto. I set off for the docks and, before noon, had succeeded in boarding the *Brickledock* as a cook's helper. I crossed the Great Lakes with my head in a galley sink full of dirty dishes, but it was great fun. In the early morning, the mate would let me visit the bridge. I would stand with my hands clutching the huge spoked wheel, my eyes glued to the compass. I was almost ready to trade my radio ambitions for a life at sea. These turned out to be five gloriously happy days I have never forgotten. Then, in the mist of an autumn morning we docked in Toronto.

The big city was not impressed with my youth and lack of experience. I persistently tracked down every program manager in every radio station. I read my practised commercials and newscast but it was soon clear to me that I was not the great new voice they had been eagerly awaiting. However, I did see Carol again. Our letters had not been nearly enough. We had missed each other deeply. We went for long walks on the campus and sat on secluded park benches. We sought out the back rows in movie theatres, where the films went largely unnoticed. Each evening she would return to the locked doors of the women's residence and I would head back to the "Y." In the morning, there would be another radio station, another audition and another refusal.

After a week or ten days, at the last Toronto radio station on my list, I decided to try the smaller towns in Ontario. One of the announcers offered to phone a colleague in Peterborough. A job was mine if I wanted it, at $125.00 per month, as a junior announcer. I accepted at once.

Once a month I took the train to Toronto and rented a cheap room I had found, a short distance from the university. It was a cold, uninviting room, with a lumpy bed, a small table and a single wooden chair. But I didn't care, since I spent as much of the weekend as possible with Carol. It was wonderful to be together but frustrating as well. There was nowhere we could be alone and private, certainly not in my room. A large notice inside the front door stated, in no uncertain terms, that ladies were not allowed in the rooms.

In Peterborough, I found a boarding house that catered to young announcers from the radio station as well as several students. As Christmas approached, I asked the landlady if she had room for Carol to stay for the holidays. She quickly agreed and we spent a glorious week together, attending holiday church services and joining the rest of the boarders in an enormous turkey dinner. We opened our simple presents and enjoyed long walks in the silent snowy streets.

Immediately after the holiday, the blow fell and I found myself once again out of work and on the street. I had stupidly crossed swords with the program manager and he fired me on the spot. So I packed my few belongings and hitchhiked from one small-town radio station to another but there were no openings. It was midwinter, very cold, and I was rapidly getting down to my few remaining dollars, with no job prospect in sight.

I was discouraged, humiliated and angry. Illogically, I blamed everyone else for the loss of my job and the dilemma I now faced. The last thing in the world I wanted to do was to return home but, with neither job nor money, there was not any alternative. I went back to Toronto and phoned my father. He agreed to wire enough money for me to take the Greyhound bus back to British Columbia.

On this day, for the first time, Carol came with me to my weekend room. We were unhappy and downhearted over our inevitable separation; everything seemed pretty hopeless to us. Carol had a couple of years at least before her studies ended and I seemed to be getting nowhere with a career. We left my place and walked the cold lonely streets of Toronto back to the university. I tried to make a brave face of it and promised I would write often. I couldn't promise to return; I really did not know where my life was going. I left Carol at her residence and returned dejectedly to my room.

The Greyhound bus journey back across the prairies and through the Rockies made no impression on me. I don't remember a day of it, although it must have been a non-stop drive of four or five days. When I arrived home, I began to think about a new career. Radio announcing was my first love but my experience in Ontario had shaken my confidence. Perhaps there wasn't a future for me in broadcasting after all. I decided to follow my father's well-meant advice. I joined the staff of the bank he had served all his working life. This was the sort of safe job he recommended.

Having failed in my own efforts to begin a career, I had decided that the least I could do was accept an offered position in the bank branch of a neighbouring town. It was a decision I soon came to regret. Once again I disappointed my father by giving up the opportunity to make a name for myself in the financial world, in favour of attending university. His concerns about my inability to settle down in a safe job were only partially lessened by my announced intention to study for the ministry of our church.

While I was trying to sort out my future, about three months after leaving Carol, she wrote saying she did not want to see me or hear from me again. I couldn't believe it. Her message was absolutely clear. She didn't even want me to reply to this, her final letter. I was shocked and hurt but it did not take long for anger to replace these initial reactions. I told myself she had met another man, perhaps a fellow student. Despite everything there had been between us, I would forget her and, somehow, get on with my life.

We did meet on one more occasion. I was home for the weekend, unaware that Carol had also returned to visit her parents. Under the circumstances, it was inevitable we would meet as, whenever we were home, we attended church to sing in the choir. I didn't realize she was there until I had entered the choir loft and looked down to the soprano section. Despite my earlier anger and my determination to forget all about her, I could hardly wait for the service to end. I rushed out the choir door and waited on the sidewalk where I knew she would have to pass. She was not happy to see me. Meeting me obviously upset her. She again made it clear to me that our relationship was over and that she did not want to see me again.

This time, I was not so vulnerable. I was again saddened by what she had said but I had to accept it. I wished her well and said goodbye, and walked home alone to my parents' house. I didn't even mention to them that I had seen Carol. In a few months, I was busy packing and looking forward to moving to Vancouver where I would attend university and begin my studies for the ministry. I did not realize then that this was yet another endeavour that was to flounder — but when it finally did, three years had passed and Carol was long forgotten.

By the time I finished telling Inge my story it had grown quite dark. The moon was high and blazing in the Mediterranean sky. We could clearly see the bright reds and oranges of the bougainvillaea that cascaded down the side of our tiny hut. Sitting on the ground leaning against the straw wall, we listened to the crickets in the tall grass under the olive trees.

"Do you know whatever happened to her?" Inge asked.

"No," I replied, "although I've often wondered about her."

"You should find out," Inge suggested. "After all, she was your first love."

This puzzled me at first but then I realized that I had fallen in love with Inge for everything she was. Just as I was not the least bit jealous of her former husband nor anyone else in her past, neither was she jealous of anyone I had met before her.

We returned to the difficult decision each of us faced and Carol was soon far from our minds. For the rest of our stay in Corfu, we returned again and again to the topic of whether we could overcome all the difficulties and end the thousands of miles separating us. Finally, we decided to take the big step. Six months later, Inge joined me in Vancouver, where we married and established a new life together. She helped me raise my three sons from my first marriage. Much to her regret, her earlier marriage had not produced children and she was forced to settle for a weekend relationship with my growing boys.

So when I returned from my prairie trip, Inge's calm reaction to what Carol had told me did not really surprise me that much. As far as she was concerned, Catherine Anne was already part of our family. To Inge, there was no choice but to find her. Nonetheless, It took several days before the significance of our situation had sunk in. We agreed there was something very deep and meaningful about a blood relationship. While marital and friendship ties could be very strong, blood relationships, even if distant and loose, were unique and somehow binding. I felt an immediate sense of responsibility toward this girl I had never met.

We talked about our right to interfere in a family that was probably quite secure and happy in its own relationships. I was deeply grateful to the man and woman who had raised my child. I wondered how they would react if I tried to find her. The most difficult question to answer was, "If you do find her, will you be able to resist making yourselves known to her?" We discussed several possible scenarios, finally deciding to take one step at a time and to trust we would know how to proceed as events unfolded.

3

The Search Begins

For several days, Inge and I could not seem to talk about anything but Catherine Anne. What kind of couple had adopted her? Where had they lived? Where did she go to school? What did she look like? Was she married? Did she have any children and was I already a grandfather? The questions went on and on. We tried to discuss only the good ones. Neither of us wanted to think of an unhappy childhood, serious illness or accident, or even a broken marriage. Even worse, there was always the chance that she was dead.

As the questions continued to grow and remain unanswered, I had to come to terms with a mounting anger. It would well up within me, often when I was alone walking along the seawall in Stanley Park or sitting in my car in traffic. I was angry with Carol for not telling me she had been pregnant and for giving up our daughter for adoption without giving me any say in her decision. I felt cheated and robbed.

I would fantasize about the possible outcome, had she shared her dilemma with me. We could have married. Under the circumstances, our parents could not have prevented us from keeping our baby. But at the same time, I knew it would have been a doomed marriage, for we were too young and immature. Even so, I then would have known my daughter and seen her grow from a tiny baby into a beautiful young woman. We would have been friends and she would have been an accepted member of my family. Instead I had been denied the love and affection of my daughter.

Yet if Carol and I had married, what about my three sons? They would not have been born. These young men were very important to me and I had a host of wonderful memories of their childhood years. Carol had a son and two other daughters as well. I knew I could not remake our lives by rewriting the history of what had happened. But why then was I so angry? I knew it was selfish anger. I wanted all the good and enjoyable experiences that might have emerged if Carol had confided in me but I shunned the emotional strain, the rejection by family and friends, the financial hardships, the reality of what would have happened to our lives.

At our final meeting outside the church, what would have happened if Carol had told me she was pregnant? For all concerned, what better solution could I have proposed than what she had already determined was best? In my anger I was judging Carol's decision in the context of today's mores and values rather than by the social reality of the 1950s.

It was startling to realize how much attitudes had changed in the thirty years between then and now. Despite the growing concern about sexually transmitted diseases, today's young men and women are no longer labelled loose and irresponsible if they indulge in sexual activity before marriage. Indeed, many parents not only condone but encourage a young couple to live together before settling down to married life. Also gone is the old belief that if a young woman becomes pregnant, she must give up her child for adoption in order to maintain the appearance of chastity.

In addition, many parents offer to provide their daughters with practical and tangible support in their pregnancy. As a result the single mother, albeit with considerable sacrifice, can often keep and support her child. If it is her decision to do so, a young mother can now provide the care and nourishment required by her child without considering adoption. It is also no longer accepted by the professionals that removing a newborn child from its mother is necessarily in the child's best interest.

An even more remarkable change is society's current attitude towards any woman who succeeds in raising and supporting her own child by herself. Not only is she no longer held in shame, she is praised and admired for her tenacity, determination and devotion. The woman herself can be extremely proud of what she has done. As to future marriage prospects, she and her friends alike hold any man in contempt who might reject her because of her baby — so much for the old notion that a woman's life will be ruined if she has by her side that constant reminder of her "immoral act."

Such were not the attitudes of the 1950s. Sex was never discussed in my home or at school. What I did manage to learn about it was from my male friends behind the back fence. Despite the reality of what I knew occurred amongst my schoolmates, premarital sexual relations were seen as immoral and sinful. I can laugh now but, thinking back, I was afraid to buy condoms, the only birth control device then available, because you had to ask the druggist for them. Not only that, he would have told my father, since they were close friends and met regularly at church.

Only when I forced myself to think back and accept the truth about attitudes of that era did my anger begin to dissipate. Thirty years ago, when Carol discovered she was pregnant, society blamed her. Anyone in her position was seen as a loose woman for not resisting male advances, no matter how persistently they were pressed. The paradox was that a young man might play around a bit — but with whom I've never quite figured out, since all the young women were supposed to say no.

Both Carol and I had grown up in church-going families and the church had very definite ideas about sin, sex and young women who got pregnant. There was tremendous pressure on them to seek anonymity and give up their babies. Adoption, to the church, was how God fulfilled his promise of rebirth for these children born in sin. Good Christian parents, longing for children of their own, could take these children into their homes and, through the rebirth of adoption, could raise them as their own offspring.

Institutions, such as the Presbyterian Home where Carol stayed, were common across the country. Here a woman could live when her pregnant condition became too noticeable. She received Christian care and was provided with both secrecy and anonymity. There was also a great deal of pressure on her from all those around her to give up her baby for adoption. Any reluctant young woman was the recipient of moral and religious persuasion which was difficult to resist. It was done in the "best interests" of all concerned. These homes found suitable parents for all their young babies. Having agreed to relinquish her child, the "loose and wayward woman" who had sinned and become pregnant became once more a lovely girl who just lacked knowledge of her sexual emotions and who, through love or ignorance, had simply made a mistake.

Carol did not have a choice. There was no support from family, friends, the church or society at large for an unmarried woman who wanted to keep her child. Her decision not to tell me about her dilemma was also made in the context of the times. Society considered the bearing of an illegitimate child to be a woman's problem. The father should not be consulted. By not informing me, Carol was only doing what was expected of her.

I realized that I had no right to be angry and, in particular, no right to be angry at Carol. Attitudes and social programs had changed dramatically over thirty years. By thinking through these things I finally rid myself of my anger and came to see just how much our society has evolved — for the better I believe.

While I was coming to terms with what Carol had done and why she had never told me about our baby, a plan began to form in my mind as to how I should go about trying to locate my daughter. There seemed to be two general directions in which to proceed. The first was lawful. The second, if not illegal, was devious and deceptive at the very least. I began by seeking a legal way of gaining access to Catherine Anne's adoption files.

As an elected member of the British Columbia legislature for six years, I had learned to decipher the legalese used by the lawyers who draft legislation. I checked the Ontario Statutes to see if I had any hope at all of obtaining information about my daughter's adoption. It was there in black and white. The law that was in place when she was born had abolished my rights as the father. The cold impersonal language was understandable to anyone: for an adoption to take place, only the mother's consent was required if a child was born out of wedlock. As the father, I had no rights at all.

From the University of BC law library, I obtained copies of all recent court decisions regarding applications to open sealed adoption records. There were not very many such cases and a recent decision seemed to close the door on any of my hopes. This particular British Columbia case involved a young man in his late twenties who was seeking access to his own adoption records. He argued that he was experiencing extreme marital problems due to "poor powers of self-perception, lack of identity, and fears of abandonment." A second reason was his need to know details of his medical and genetic past. The man was a deep-sea diver and he sought his natural parents' medical backgrounds so that he would be able to anticipate any medical problems both in connection with his work and also in case he chose to father children.

The judge ruled that the man's alleged reasons for his marital problems were not sufficient justification to open the records. As to the man's fears about his deep-sea diving job or possible fatherhood, the judge ruled that events that might or might not occur in the future were also insufficient reason to let him examine his adoption file. This same case dealt with something that I had never come across before. The more I thought about it the more I began to question the logic of the secrecy surrounding adoption .

Some Canadian provinces provide that adoption does not remove a child's right of inheritance from its natural parents. Like all natural children, the adopted child may claim certain rights in regard to the provisions of a parent's will. However, in most cases, the adopted child does not know the identity of his natural parents. What a paradox: an adopted child may inherit from its natural parents but the child cannot be told who his parents are. Only politicians and lawyers could have produced such non-sense. Nonetheless, the judge in the BC case stated, "In my view the possibility of gaining inheritance from natural parents can hardly be deemed 'good cause'...." The finding stands as a precedent but, significantly, not without some dissent.

In a 1985 Prince Edward Island case dealing with a similar application, the judge stated:

> It cannot be said that the right was given in a vacuum. Neither can it be said that the rights of the natural parents or kindred to inherit from the adopted child were given in a vacuum. A person who does not know who her natural parents or kindred are cannot expect to inherit from them unless some contact is made. The only contact that would have any worthwhile effect would be through information obtained from the adoption file.
>
> Since the legislature provided for inheritance by both the adopted child and the natural parents, it cannot be assumed that it gave such a right while

on the other hand preventing the affected parties from determining if they, in fact, had an inheritance due to them.

This same judge attacked the earlier decision of the BC judge who had ruled that records should not be opened just because a medical problem, inherited from natural parents, might appear sometime in the future:

> In my opinion such a definitive statement does not properly recognize the right of an adopted person nor does it recognize current medical facts. It is a well known medical fact that diabetes is hereditary. It is further a known fact that where there is a history of diabetes, proper diet can lessen the possibility of acquiring the disease. To say to a person that theycannot obtain information of their natural parents until they have acquired the disease would be locking the door after the horse has escaped.

Other facts convinced the PEI judge that there were enough reasons for him to order the adoption files opened and he said: "The applicant is an adult and should have the right to know her heritage. She did not ask to be born into this world, but being born neither her natural parents nor her adoptive parents should have the right to keep her uninformed of her background." Yet comments about the apparent inequity or stupidity of the existing law were just that, comments only, with no precedent-setting capacity. The balance of my research indicated that Canadian courts had heard few applications for the opening of adoption records. Furthermore, except for the PEI case of 1985, the courts had rejected all such applications.

On top of my own interpretation of the law, I instructed my lawyer to give me an opinion whether the court, in a case such as mine, might grant me access to my daughter's file. It was no surprise when he advised me that my situation was unique. There was no record of a father in my circumstances making any such application to the courts. However, with regard to the cases I had already examined, he advised that any attempt I made to proceed by this route would, in all probability, end in failure. As well, he reminded me of one of the glaring inequities in our legal system. In a precedent-setting case such as this, I would be opposed by a battery of government-paid lawyers in hearings that would probably end up before the Supreme Court of Canada. Taxpayers would pay for the government lawyers while I, a lone citizen, would have to finance my side of the case out of my own pocket. This has been true in many cases involving civil rights, including those concerning adoption.

While my lawyer was pondering my chances in the courts, I had already begun official inquiries into the location of any records about my daughter. Somewhere in Ontario, there was a record of Catherine Anne's birth as well as the details of her adoption. People told me I was lucky that my daughter's adoption took place in Ontario. Apparently, records there were in much better shape than those in some of the other provinces. I was not convinced of this on the basis of my first inquiries. Any information about my daughter seemed to have disappeared into the labyrinths of bureaucracy.

I wrote to the Ontario Ministry of Community and Social Services, which now had jurisdiction over all adoption files in that province. I could not believe it when they informed me that they had no record of either Catherine Anne's birth or her adoption. Unless I could do better than this, my search was doomed to an early end. I asked them to search their files again.

Weeks passed before I received any news. When their letter eventually arrived it simply informed me that they had asked for the assistance of the Children's Aid Society of Metropolitan Toronto. My daughter's file was obviously still missing. More weeks passed and then the

Children's Aid Society informed me: "We have checked our records with the information supplied and have not been able to locate your daughter's file."

What was going on here? Carol remembered well all the details of Catherine Anne's birth and adoption. She had lived with the doubts and guilt all these years. Now, when we wanted to discover what had happened to our daughter, how could her records simply disappear? The search continued and the Society wrote again:

> We checked with the Child Welfare Branch to assure ourselves that your child had been adopted, but they were unable to find any record of an adoption in Ontario.
>
> Wondering if it were possible that the adoption took place in another province, we checked with the office of the Registrar General which should have shown that the original birth registration had been replaced by the adoption registration. We found instead that there was no registration of birth at all for Catherine Anne. This leaves us with many questions and we are attempting to do some follow-up through Women's College Hospital and the Presbyterian Church. Unfortunately, the home no longer exists, but we are hoping that their records may have been retained in some church office.

Even though I was having trouble getting my search started, some things were clear. None of them made me very happy. Despite Ontario's reputation in this area, birth and adoption records were not very efficient. Also, there now seemed to be a chance that Catherine Anne's adoption had involved a family from outside Ontario. If that was so, how would I ever find her? Officials in Toronto had not even been able to find birth records for my daughter, let alone any details about her adoption.

It appeared that my hopes now lay with the slim chance that some church worker at the Presbyterian Home might have held onto the records of children placed for adoption through that agency. No wonder I had heard so many sad stories from others who had their hopes dashed by missing, inaccurate or destroyed records.

My troubles were not over yet. Two more months passed before I again heard from Children's Aid. The social worker assigned to the case reported: "I have continued to pursue the Presbyterian Church in an attempt to locate records from the home ... but this has been without results. It would appear that these records have been destroyed or lost and no one today has any knowledge of their whereabouts."

The search for church records having proved fruitless, the ministry officials now asked the hospital for help. This time, mechanical failure and even an ill-timed Canadian postal strike intervened against me: "We were held up in our pursuit of hospital records through a broken film reader and lack of follow through by their staff, who had promised to telephone us when they had read the records, but instead wrote a letter which sat until the end of the strike."

This time, however, there was some good news as well. That letter, delayed by the postal strike, went on state that the hospital records "... confirm the birth at least and notes that your daughter was 'Discharged to foster parents through the Presbyterian Home' on October 15, 1952."

At first, I thought that this statement raised the possibility that Catherine Anne had not been adopted after all, and instead, may have ended up in a foster home. However, I later learned the terms adoptive parents and foster parents were often used interchangeably in those days. At least I now had confirmation of Catherine Anne's birth.

More weeks passed and then came the long-awaited information. At long last, the file had been found. The ministry's letter read: "The only file we could locate both here and at Metro Children's Aid Society when you first inquired contained just one form which was signed by Carol and which did not identify the baby's Christian name. Records of adoptees are filed under the adoptive name and unfortunately our cross reference system broke down on this case."

Looking back, I suppose it was nothing more than an administrative glitch that had delayed the location of the file. For a time, however, I feared that those who had arranged for my daughter's adoption had lost all record of her. During this time, I had been unable to prove that Catherine Anne even existed.

4

By Lawful Means

Now that the ministry officials had found the file, there did not seem to be any point in making a fuss about the whole thing. They had found it and that was what mattered. But I received yet another setback when that same file revealed that Carol had not named me as the father of Catherine Anne. Thirty years before, lying in her hospital bed, she had decided to keep my identity secret. She left blank the space on the birth registration for the father's name. Under the circumstances, the ministry would not divulge any information to me. In fairness, I could only agree with them — there was no way they could tell whether I was the father of this child or some nosey relative or neighbour snooping around.

At my request, Carol wrote the social worker who was dealing with my inquiries, informing her I was, indeed, the father. All of this took time and only after phone calls from Carol did she decide my inquiries were proper. She was now willing to reveal to me what the file contained, which she admitted was very little. the Presbyterian Home for Unwed Mothers had indeed arranged the adoption. The new parents had accepted the baby at the hospital where she was born. Finally, she assured me that they were a "good couple." That was it. Any other information she had was considered to be identifying and, therefore, secret.

A conscientious social worker today takes detailed medical records and background history from both natural parents. When

identifying details have been removed, a summary of the information is given to the adopting parents. In general terms, therefore, the parents know a fair amount about the baby they are adopting. Likewise, the files usually contain a background report about the adopting parents. A social worker will make this available to the birth mother, should she request it. Some time later the adopted child may receive non-identifying background information about her birth parents from those same files.

I will never know whether the original worker in charge of my daughter's case was simply inefficient and careless or whether the practice of the Presbyterian Home and Children's Aid Society at that time was just plain cold and thoughtless. In fact, if I was to believe what I was being told, Catherine Anne's file contained nothing by way of background information about her adopting parents other than the assessment of the social worker who met them that they were a "good couple." The ministry did provide one other piece of information. But it only served to increase my anger about the whole adoption jungle I had entered.

I was informed that there had been no further contact between the worker assigned to the case and Catherine Anne or her new parents. Thus, the agency which had arranged for the transfer of a baby girl from the arms of her natural mother to those of her adoptive mother had never once assessed how this vulnerable human being was adapting to her new environment.

It was now clear to me that I was going to get very little information about my daughter from these people, who did not even know whether she was alive or dead.

I was invited to submit my name to the newly formed Ontario Adoption Disclosure Registry, the first such agency in the country. Governments have since set up similar registries in all but one of the provinces, and in that province too plans are in place to follow the others' lead. More than anything else, the creation of these facilities acknowledges that countless thousands of parents and children have rejected the old theories about adoption secrecy. They demand to know the truth about themselves. Unfortunately, the reality is that these registries also represent government's refusal to address the real issue — the adoptees' demands for automatic right of access to their files.

When Carol and I responded by registering our names, I was not very hopeful. When I first learned about it, I thought that the reunion registry was a great idea, holding the promise of an early and successful conclusion to my search. In theory, it made sense. If Catherine Anne had also registered, and providing her adoptive mother and father had no objection, the reunion registry would arrange communication between us. However, I sadly discovered that the registry does not function as simply as that.

The rules vary in each province, but most of these registries are simply a depository of consents — that is, subject to the usual bureaucratic delays and mistakes, if all parties to an adoption submit their desire for reunion, they will be notified by the registry. Communication between them can then begin. There are, however, major problems with this system that make it totally useless to most applicants.

First, not everyone party to an adoption will have heard of the registry or have any motivation to enter their names. This can be true even if they do not object to reunion. Furthermore, the adoptive parents may never have told the child of his or her adoption. Another difficulty arises when, unknown to all others in the adoption triangle, one party may have moved far away or died. Dozens of combinations of events and circumstances can dash any hope of reunion through the adoption registry.

At the time I registered, Ontario's registry would not undertake any search for my daughter to see if she desired to meet her natural father, because she had not registered herself. While the rules in that province have since changed somewhat, there are still only three provinces that will conduct any form of a search and, even then, these are carried out under very restrictive conditions.

The other major hurdle I faced was the registry's demand that Catherine Anne's adoptive parents also agree to any reunion. I had absolutely no way of knowing what their feelings might be toward the idea of the girl they had raised as their own daughter meeting her natural parents. Furthermore, since all concerned were now mature adults, should they, or Carol, or myself for that matter, be able to stand in the way of a reunion desired by all the rest? Again, the various provincial registries differ about whether one or both of the adoptive parents must consent to reunion.

It is easy to imagine the anger and frustration that results when such consent is unobtainable. I had already met an adoptee, a woman now in her fifties, whose natural parents had agreed to a reunion. Her adoptive father had died but her adoptive mother, now almost eighty, refused to grant permission for the reunion. There was absolutely nothing the registry staff could do but close the file until the old lady died. This refusal was hardly likely to enhance whatever feelings remained between that lady and her adopted daughter. There was every reason to believe that vindictive motives were at the heart of her decision.

I also discovered that the few registries that do initiate a search will not do so on behalf of a natural parent such as myself. I could register in the hope that my daughter had done the same but only she could start a search. Likewise, siblings and grandparents have few rights. Only a few of the registries will recognize grandparents or guardians in circumstances where the parents have died or are incompetent.

It is particularly frustrating for brothers and sisters of the adopted. Few reunion registries will recognize their right of reunion. There are an unknown number of cases, probably in the thousands, where brothers and sisters have ended up adopted into different homes. It is easy to understand why they would seek reunion. Yet the registry is of little use to them.

Nova Scotia has tried to respond to another dilemma. What to do about all the women to whom they once promised absolute confidentiality? When the government set up a registry in 1984, it created two classes of adoptions. The registry would be passive regarding all adoptions that took place before its establishment. It would arrange a reunion only when all parties to the adoption desired one. In more recent adoptions, the registry would actively help an adult adoptee try to find his or her natural parents. How the Nova Scotia government rationalizes this policy in terms of the equality rights of the children involved is a mystery.

Another area in which the registries differ from one another is the provision of counselling. In a few provinces counselling is mandatory and the registry will not arrange a reunion unless all parties are willing to receive such help and advice. But hardly any of them maintain the highly skilled staff needed to deal with a situation in which one individual is reluctant or refuses to consent to reunion, despite the strong desire of all the others. One instance is a case in which a child and his natural mother both eagerly seek reunion, with the support of the adoptive parents. However, the natural father may refuse to acknowledge his paternity if the mother named the father on the original birth documents but never informed him of the pregnancy. Such situations require experienced counselling skills.

Although I reluctantly concluded that I would receive little help or information from the Ontario Adoption Disclosure Registry, I nevertheless waited eagerly to hear from them. Requesting such a registry search can, frequently, be one of the early frustrations in a reunion attempt. Like any other government office, efficiency is directly related to the supply of adequate staff. Many provinces with registries have failed to provide the personnel necessary to respond promptly to search requests. Backlogs are the norm. One can wait several months before receiving a reply to a letter, let alone getting action on a specific request.

Fortunately, I made my submission to the Ontario Registry when the lineup was fairly short. As a result, within a matter of a few weeks, I received the news I had expected. There was no request for reunion from my daughter. Despite what I had already learned about the registry and its apparent weaknesses, I discovered that I had built up my hopes. This, the first of many disappointments to come, caught me unprepared. I considered giving up, since it appeared that Catherine Anne did not wish to know about me or her mother.

A few days later, I was taking my usual early morning walk on the seawall and I had stopped to rest and soak up the sounds and sights of the sea. I watched the ravens and crows scratching amongst the rocks for their breakfast. In that peaceful and reassuring setting, I realized that I was letting myself give up too easily.

Catherine Anne might be totally unaware of her adoption. What if her parents had never told her? If she did know, had she heard of the registry? What if her family had long ago left the province? Chances were fairly good that she no longer lived in Ontario. How, then, would she know of the registry? No one was going to look in her file or find her. No one was going to ask her if she would welcome a reunion with her natural mother and father. If I wanted to find my daughter, I was going to have to start searching, just like all the other people I had met were doing.

With legal avenues apparently closed to me, there seemed to be no alternative but to embark upon less orthodox measures. I began by contacting some of the leaders of the adoption reform movement in Vancouver. I knew who they were, as I had interviewed them on several occasions for my radio talk show. In this respect I was fortunate because much of the current demand for adoption reform has arisen from the early activities of a small group of activist women in British Columbia. Their efforts eventually led to the formation of such groups as Parent Finders, now with affiliated offices right across Canada. Many of them had either conducted successful searches themselves or were in the midst of an active search. They were more than willing to share their experiences and show me how to begin my own search. In addition, I went to our local library and borrowed all the recent books on adoption, including a couple aimed specifically at how to search for blood relatives.

The first thing I learned was that there was no easy way to conduct a search. There were a few stories about how a cooperative social worker left an adoption file open on the desk while absent from the room, but these were the exception. What I required were countless records and bits and pieces of information, in the hope that some pattern or clue would emerge. I would need a lot of time and patience. I read of women searching for an adopted child for ten and twenty years without success. I now also knew that I was not going to get any help in my search from any of the official sources which might have information that would be of great assistance to me. Indeed, all government agencies would actively oppose my efforts, and even do everything in their power to prevent my success.

I interviewed scores of searchers and learned of the tricks and mild deception used to get by the keepers of hidden records. One woman simply phoned the hospital where she knew she was born and requested medical information from her file, since she was now pregnant herself. Much to her surprise and pleasure the hospital told her she was the only female baby born there that day. They even told her the name of her mother.

The adoptive mother of another woman told her the name of the doctor who had attended her natural mother. This same doctor had arranged for her adoption. Since he was still in practice, she made an appointment to see him. Needless to say, he was shocked and surprised at her request for information.

Another woman knew her natural mother's name and that she was living in the United States at the time of her birth. Patiently, state by state, she was in the process of examining telephone and city directories of every American town and city. She wrote everyone with that name to inquire if they knew her mother. Slowly, year by year, she was covering every state, although so far without success.

A simple phone call to the Department of Vital Statistics provided another woman with enough information to make her search easy. She gave one of the clerks the story that she was looking after a will and was trying to locate the address of a woman named as a beneficiary. She purposely played it rather innocent and dumb. After the clerk asked her to hang on for a few minutes he came back on the line saying, "Here it is and, by the way, you didn't get this information from me."

At first, one of the most common and successful ruses was for a woman to write for a birth certificate, pretending to be the birth mother. Another searcher told me how she had requested her mother's birth certificate without mentioning the word adoption at all. Instead, she said she was a Mormon and required the documentation for a "Purification of the Soul" ceremony. It worked and she was able to complete her search successfully.

She told me of others who successfully located their natural parents only to discover unpleasant or unhappy details of their origin. The reality at the end of a search is often not what the dreams are about. The finale to a long and exhausting drama is frequently disappointment and letdown. Likewise, not everyone wants to learn about their birth parents, and are content instead to live within the embrace of their adopted family.

"What you need is a skip tracer," said one lady who had been searching for her adopted daughter's natural parents for over five years. She had laboriously gone through hundreds of newspapers and city directories trying to get a current address for the woman she was seeking. Finally, in frustration, she asked for help from a friend who was a skip tracer. This person's regular job was tracking down bad debtors. He obviously had knowledge of methods unavailable to the rest of us, because he was successful in his assignment in just a couple of days.

The determination and ingenuity of another woman really impressed me. She knew her birth date and the city where she was born. She examined the microfilms of the newspaper birth announcements. There she discovered the names of three women who had given birth to babies on that same date. She contacted them all and asked if they remembered other women on the maternity ward with them who had their babies the same day. As it turned out, all of them recalled her mother but none knew her name. It hurt her to learn from them that her mother seemed very sad and alone in the hospital.

These stories were helpful and provided me with all sorts of ideas for my own search. Unfortunately, I also learned that most government employees who had charge of the records and files that would be so valuable to me were well aware of all the tricks. Searchers before me had tried most of the stratagems and the social workers and file clerks were unlikely to be fooled by any attempts I might make.

Ironically, my attempt to find my daughter was not the first search I had conducted for lost family relatives. Many years before, when I was in my early twenties, I had left university to experience a different kind of education. I wandered around Europe with a rucksack on my back and met hundreds of young men and women from other countries. Together, we marvelled at Europe's history and culture, which we had previously only read about. I had brought with me a copy of the frontispiece of our old family bible, which listed forebears on my mother's side of the family. All my grandparents had cut all ties with their relatives when they emigrated.

My mother had heard many stories of how her grandmother had come from Scotland and she treasured romantic notions of the family clan. While travelling through Inverness, I decided to stop for a few days and see if I could find any trace of my mother's relatives. At the city hall, officials were more than willing to pore through old books and records. They finally located the death notice of my great grandmother, listing her next of kin. From that it was easy to locate living relatives, second cousins to the branch of the family that was now in Canada.

Memories of that earlier search came back to me now but this time I was not liable to get the same sort of cooperation from government officials. Under no circumstance would they grant me free access to the books and files that might quickly provide me with the information I was seeking. There was only one option. Whereas my Scottish investigations had been proper and legitimate, my search for my daughter would lead me to enlist in an underground movement. I joined a group of thousands of otherwise law-abiding Canadians who, by whatever means necessary, were determined to find their lost families.

5

An Interviewer's Trick

Before embarking on my clandestine search, I considered what information I would require to begin. Once again I realized how little I knew about my daughter. Although her adoption had taken place in Ontario, I had no way of knowing if the adopting parents were from that province. They could have travelled right across the country to get a baby.

Even if I had known where they lived at the time of the adoption, I had no way of knowing where they now resided. Furthermore, considering the way people move around in Canada, there was every chance that Catherine Anne and her new family had moved to a different city or province. Then another disheartening thought struck me. She could have moved to the United States, Europe, Australia — to any country in the world. My task seemed hopeless.

As a first priority, I would have to narrow down my search, but how to do this was my first challenge. My questions and plans lay untouched for several days as I tried to determine where to start. Finally I told myself to stop worrying about everything I did not know and concentrate instead on what I did know.

I wrote down Catherine Anne's birth date, Oct. 7, 1952. I knew she was born in Women's College Hospital, Toronto, so that came next. Carol had stayed at the Presbyterian Home for Unwed Mothers. That might prove important, so it also went on my list. In reality that was all I knew to be true. Therefore, I would have to begin by trying to enlarge upon that basic information.

Thus far, I had not accomplished very much by writing a lot of letters. Perhaps if I met personally with those in charge of the ministry's adoption records, I would be able to get more information upon which to base my search. Seven months had elapsed since I first heard the news from Carol, and I had unearthed hardly a thing. I decided to take a leave from my radio talk show in Vancouver. I would go to Toronto, visit the Ministry of Community and Social Services and meet face to face with those who had been responding to my inquiries.

Others told me that people who worked in the adoption records department of government were quite reluctant to meet people like me. Perhaps it was easier to lie or say no by letter. Over the years, I had learned much about communicating with government. When I served as Rentalsman for the Province of British Columbia, I was responsible for resolving all landlord-tenant disputes. In that capacity I learned of the countless delaying devices and the lexicon of excuses available to a bureaucrat.

Coming from the outside, I had impressed upon my staff the need for open communication with those seeking our help. Frequently, I had exercised my managerial authority to override the habit of bureaucratic evasion. Above all, I had learned that the more official-sounding the message and the more authoritative the writer, the more willingly came a response. Public servants want to avoid, if at all possible, citizens going over their heads to their political masters.

My requests for appointments, therefore, were made in formal language, professionally typed on personal stationery. I made frequent reference to my position as a radio talk show host and former member of the British Columbia legislature. In each case, there was a follow-up phone call from my secretary. Handwritten letters couched in timid phrases usually do not, I am sorry to say, produce the kind of reaction I received. In their responses, the ministry's officials said that they would be happy to meet with me.

I spent every minute of the flight to Toronto preparing for my interviews. I carefully made a list of questions for each person I would meet. These questions had to be exactly the right ones and I had to listen carefully to the answers. I knew that the most helpful information might come from a chance or offhand remark. I considered using a tape recorder, but decided that that might be too intimidating. I would have to rely on my memory and notes.

My first meeting was with the woman responsible for the care and keeping of adoption files and records. The office had just opened when she showed me into a tiny room, barely large enough for a desk and two chairs. There certainly was not an open file folder on this desk; there was not so much as a piece of paper lying around. I sat down, noting the cold atmosphere created by the drab civil service decor. "How can I help you?" she asked.

"First," I replied, "I would like you to satisfy me that there really is a file for my daughter and that, should she inquire, you will give her my name and address."

The woman apologized for the earlier delay in locating the file and offered a meaningless explanation for the mix-up. "We eventually found it in the basement," she said, "filed under the mother's maiden name."

I let that pass and asked her, "What exactly does the file contain?"

"The file contains Catherine Anne's original birth certificate, a note that a social worker interviewed her mother, and the adoption documents themselves which identify the new parents."

Not a very thick file, I thought and, as I suspected, not a word about any follow-up visit or any check on the baby's well-being.

"What can you tell me about the adopting parents?" I asked.

She examined her notes, the actual file obviously not being in the office, and explained, "I can't tell you anything that might help you in any way to identify the parents. However, I can tell you that the father was a professional and in his early forties. The couple did not have any other children at the time of adoption."

She also reported that the adopting parents had visited the hospital themselves to pick up the baby.

"Were they from Ontario?" I asked.

"I cannot reveal that," she quickly replied.

I recalled a letter she had sent me earlier in which she had said that she was checking to see if my daughter's adoption had taken place outside the province. This was at the time when the ministry was having difficulty locating Catherine Anne's files. I reminded her of this correspondence and repeated my question. "Were you able to determine whether the adoption took place in Ontario?"

"Yes," she stated, "but I can't tell you whether or not it did."

"I must conclude from what you are saying or, rather, what you are not saying that the parents were from Ontario. You also are implying the final court approval of my daughter's adoption took place in Ontario."

She looked hard at me but said nothing.

"Were the parents from Toronto?" I asked.

"No."

"Did they live in a large city or a town?" I continued.

She thought for a moment and then said, "A small town. I cannot tell you any more than that."

I decided not to press further on that point. However, I noted that she would probably not have known the information she had given me about the size of the town unless it was in Ontario. With that probable conclusion, I changed the direction of my questioning.

"Were they Protestant or Roman Catholic?" I continued.

"I cannot say," she said.

"Were they made aware of the mother's request that her daughter receive a musical education?"

"I cannot be certain of that," she responded. Then she added, "Under the circumstances, it would be normal practice for the parents to be told of the mother's wishes in that regard."

"But there's nothing on the file?" I asked.

"No."

"What else can you tell me?"

"Nothing."

She had come to the end of her notes and this was all the information I was going to receive. I realized that the woman was only doing her job and had taken an oath not to answer the very questions I was asking. However, that was not helping me in my search so I resorted to the interviewer's trick of righteous indignation. Raising my voice, I stated angrily, "Surely, at the very least, you can tell me where the court documents are. At what court can I make application to have them examined by a judge? I am simply not satisfied with the answers you have given me!"

She was quite startled by my performance and stuttered, "Well, they'd be in … let me think … Wellington County … they'd be in the Guelph Courthouse."

I abandoned my assumed anger and quickly thanked her for her help and cooperation. I did not want to reveal to her the significance of what she had just told me. Within moments, I left her office.

Outside the government building, I made notes of everything I had learned. It was not very much but I now knew that court approval of the adoption had taken place in the Guelph Courthouse. That must mean the adopting parents lived, at the time, in Wellington County. I was now certain that the adoption had taken place in Ontario.

Mixed feelings ran through me. The meeting had left me with a sense of frustration. I was angry that a government employee, someone who had no connection with me or my family, had access to knowledge denied to me. While she refused to tell me, she knew the answers to all the questions I had asked. Furthermore, she knew the actual names of the adopting parents and where they had lived at the time. She had in her hand the very facts that would have ended my search almost immediately. To me, she personified a government telling me it knew better than I did what information I should have about my own daughter.

As I stood on the sidewalk outside that building, I even contemplated ways of breaking in and examining the files myself. I knew I was being ridiculous but I thought about it nonetheless. Instead, I walked up the street rather aimlessly, thinking about what the woman had told me. By responding the way she did to my display of temper she had inadvertently narrowed my search to the province of Ontario.

Later, when I returned to Vancouver, I wrote to this woman and expressed my deep concern over how little she had been able to tell me. My letter expressed my frustration and anger. I hoped it might prompt her to tell me more about my daughter and the people who had adopted her. After thanking her for having agreed to see me, I stated:

> My daughter was placed for adoption without my knowledge or consent but with the consent of the mother, which was all that was required at that time. The mother's decision was based on certain advice and assurance given her at the time by persons authorized by the Government of Ontario to give such advice.
>
> On the basis of the information made available to me, the baby was given to adoptive parents at the hospital. No one seems to know who arranged the adoption. No one seems to know whether the family was interviewed or investigated in any way.

Despite the wishes of the mother, it does not appear that the baby's given names were recorded, let alone made known to the adopting parents. Again, despite the mother's specific request, it appears no attempt was made to see that the baby was assured an opportunity to pursue a musical education. In short, from the moment the baby was handed over, there was no official contact whatsoever.

I concluded my letter by suggesting: "… if this adoption was being considered today, far more information about the adopting parents would be provided than I am now seeking. How then can you justify denying me the little information you do possess?"

She replied to my letter, defending her silence by quoting the legislative prohibitions against the release of any more information than she had already given me. This was to be my final contact with ministry officials. It was clear that they were not going to provide me with further assistance. Furthermore, I knew that if they could, they would hinder any attempts I made to locate my daughter.

The weather in Toronto was cold but sunny as I continued my walk after my first meeting. Although I had seldom returned to Toronto, I began to recognize the buildings and streets. I had more than an hour before my next appointment so I kept walking. I did not stop until I stood outside the school where I used to leave Carol after our weekends together. The building did not appear to have changed much, as I even found the residence door where we stood in the shadows and said our good-byes.

The sounds were the same. From open windows I could hear the pianos, violins and clarinets of the students at practice. The jangle of mixed instruments blended with the outside traffic to produce a cacophony of sound that brought back a flood of memories. I remembered a dance I had attended with Carol in a large hall inside the building. I even recalled a similar cold winter's day when, together, we had watched the Santa Claus Parade, which was then one of the biggest parades I had ever seen.

I knew there was not much point in it, but I continued walking toward Women's College Hospital. I stood outside the building, this time only imagining what had occurred there so long ago. In my earlier radio interviews, I had heard first-hand of the heartbreak so many women felt at not knowing what had happened to the baby they had given up for adoption. Carol was one of them.

As I stood on the sidewalk outside the hospital, I felt discouraged by how little I knew about Catherine Anne. All I had learned was that, from the moment she left this hospital, there was no record of anyone ever checking about whether she was healthy, happy or well-cared for. No one even knew if she was still alive.

6

Bluff and Deception

My next Toronto appointment was with an official of the Children's Aid Society. She confirmed that her agency had supervised the adoption procedures. She also said their files indicated that one of their workers had visited Carol at the Presbyterian Home. Beyond that, she volunteered no further information. I thought I would test what I had learned earlier in the day. "They told me at the ministry that the final court approval of the adoption took place in Guelph," I said. I then asked, "Can you tell me if your records also show this?"

She was clearly startled by my knowledge of this fact and replied, "Oh, I would never have told you that. I'm surprised they gave you that information."

She had given me the confirmation I sought. She clearly knew that the Guelph court had approved the adoption, and considered that the information would help me in identifying the adoptive parents.

Deciding to press her on this point, I said, "I must assume therefore that it was the Children's Aid Society in Guelph that did the home studies before they approved the adoption. Am I correct?"

She did not answer for a moment and then replied, "I'm not prepared to say. I can't say."

I fought to control the anger rising within me. Here was the second person I had met today who had all the information I needed to find Catherine Anne. I was older, and presumably more mature, than either of them yet they were denying me information about my own flesh and blood. Furthermore, it was plain they both felt they were acting properly and in the best interest of everyone involved.

The rest of our interview was awkward. Obviously, as an experienced social worker, this woman was very concerned that I had been given information that might prove helpful to my investigation. She also clearly sensed my determination to find my daughter. Concerned by this, she felt it necessary to warn me of the harm I might cause if I continued on my course. "You could disrupt a very happy family," she said. "Do you have any idea how much harm you may cause?"

"I believe I understand what you mean," I replied. "But what makes you so sure you are right? How many adoption reunions have you seen, and how many were regretted?"

"There haven't been that many. However, many adopting parents are afraid of just what you are doing now."

"I am fully aware of that. It's something I know I must consider but it has absolutely nothing to do with my search, let alone my daughter's right to know the truth about herself. For the moment, I simply want to know if she's alive and well."

"You won't stop there. Once you've found her you'll want to meet her."

"What if I find her and she's in trouble and I'm able to help her? Should I simply ignore her and walk away?"

"I don't know. I just don't think you should go on with your search," she stated.

"I hadn't thought a lot about these questions before I knew I had a daughter," I said. "While I appreciate your concerns, I am becoming more and more convinced that the whole adoption system is crazy. It's artificial and contrived, protected by secrecy, and everyone's afraid to touch it because they don't know what would happen if they did. What about the children? How can you possibly know that it's in their best interest to cut them off forever from their natural roots?"

She looked at me sadly. "I hope you know what you're doing," she said.

"I'm not absolutely sure I do," I replied. "I just know I must continue to try to find my daughter."

I liked her. She was forthright and honest. I believe she knew that the system she had worked in all her life was beginning to come apart. Because vulnerable human beings were involved, she was very worried and I respected that. I left, somewhat disturbed by our conversation but determined more than ever to continue my search. For the moment, I pushed aside the concerns she had raised. I would deal with them later.

Returning to my hotel, I assessed the significance of what I had learned. My most important discovery was that the adoption had taken place in Ontario. I had also determined that the final court approval of the adoption had taken place in Guelph. I was pretty certain, although not absolutely sure, that the Guelph Children's Aid Society had been the responsible agency, probably doing a home study of the adopting parents. If I could confirm this, I could assume with reasonable safety that the family lived, at the time, in Ontario's Wellington County, since that was the area of jurisdiction of that particular agency. It had been a far more productive day than I had expected.

My trip was already paying significant dividends. I had feared that my quest would take me from Newfoundland to British Columbia. Even worse, the possibility had existed that the adopting parents lived in the United States. But now, a few pieces of the puzzle were fitting together. I had learned from earlier inquiries that organizations such as the Presbyterian Home for Unwed Mothers seldom arranged out-of-province adoptions. Furthermore, I had also determined that it was normal procedure for final court approval of an adoption to take place in the county where the child was living at the time. Everything pointed to Ontario and it was beginning to look as though I would be able to further narrow my search to one county. It was time to rent a car, go to Guelph and see what I could find out.

My drive through the beautiful Ontario countryside was invigorating because, for the first time, I felt I was making real progress. I looked forward to what I might discover in Guelph. My first stop was the local office of the Children's Aid Society. Here, I would have to use a great deal of bluff. If I could confirm that this office had supervised the adoption, then all my assumptions about the adopting family having lived in Wellington County would be proven right. I decided not to tell them I was Catherine Anne's father.

In a very clipped and businesslike manner I asked the receptionist if I could please talk to someone who could advise me regarding the Society's role in an adoption of a certain child. She took me into an office where a young woman asked if she could be of assistance. I said, "I am making inquiries about the circumstances surrounding an adoption which took place here some years ago. I simply wish to determine if this office was the supervising agency."

Much to my surprise, she simply asked if I had the original name of the child concerned and the year of the adoption. This I supplied, whereupon she asked me to wait in her office while she checked the files. She returned within ten minutes saying, "Isn't that interesting? I see that our Toronto office was inquiring about this same file a few weeks ago."

My heart jumped as I realized that the Toronto office, in all probability, had been trying to locate Catherine Anne's file as a result of my earlier inquiries.

"Yes," she continued, "this branch did supervise the adoption but the actual file contents have been sent to our Toronto office."

Mumbling my thanks for her cooperation, I left immediately, suggesting there would be more formal inquiries now that I had confirmed that this was the supervising office I had been seeking. I had done it. I now knew for certain that the Guelph Children's Aid Society had been in charge of the adoption formalities and that their jurisdiction covered all of Wellington County.

While driving along the freeway, I had been plotting a possible strategy for my search. It had depended on my being able to confine my efforts to a specific area. This I felt I could now do. The court that granted final approval to Catherine Anne's adoption had sat in Guelph. The local Children's Aid Society had been the supervising agency. I had been able to confirm what I had learned earlier in Toronto. I was certain the adopting parents had resided in Wellington County at the time they took my daughter into their home.

The plan that was beginning to crystallize in my mind was to prepare two lists. The first would contain all the names of those girls from Wellington County who might be Catherine Anne. The second list would be the names of all the men who could possibly be her adoptive father. By cross referencing the two lists, I could eliminate all those girls whose surnames were not one on my list of possible fathers. If I was lucky, this would produce a short list of girls' names. Against such a list I could apply Catherine Anne's birth date, something I had and knew to be correct.

In theory, my plan just might produce the adoptive name of my daughter and where she first lived. However, I still had to collect all the names I would need for my two lists. I thought about all the places that would have kept records of girls living in the county. Her new parents must have taken her to see a doctor. He would have kept records, but I saw no chance of getting my hands on them. Likewise, the hospitals in the area would carefully guard such information. If Catherine Anne had been baptized, the church involved might have records, but I would have to visit every church in the county to find out. My best bet seemed to be the local schools.

Remembering countless parents' nights I had attended for my sons, I knew all schools kept voluminous records on every child that had ever sat in their classrooms. Those records included names, birthdays, parents' names, addresses — everything I could possible require for the preparation of my girls' list. However, there was one significant flaw in this scheme. I would have to make the assumption that the family stayed in the county until Catherine Anne began attending school at the age of six. This was a gamble, but people did not move around as much in 1952 as they do today. It also seemed safe to bet that a couple adopting their first child would be settled in a community. The schools seemed to be the place to begin, but would I be allowed to have their registration lists?

The next morning before leaving the hotel, I looked through the Guelph telephone directory and located the offices of the Wellington County Board of Education. At the reception desk, I suggested that I was doing some historical research into students who had attended schools in the area some years before. I was happy to learn that there was a historical officer and that she could see me immediately. She turned out to be a delightful retired school teacher whose responsibility was the impossible task of trying to sort out the mounds of material dating back to the early days of organized public education in the county.

It was a great relief to discover that she was not the least bit concerned with my credentials or my reasons for research. My interest in the history of the old schools was enough for her. She provided me with an overview of the school system and confirmed that the Board of Education boundaries matched those of Wellington County and had not changed since 1952.

She took me into a back room filled from floor to ceiling with shelves, each crammed with boxes of file cards. I had mentioned to her that the years I was interested in were around 1958, which was the year Catherine Anne would have begun her schooling. She began to move the boxes around, glancing at the handwritten labels as she pushed them aside. "Some of those early records were destroyed in a fire many years ago but a lot of them are still here. You can look at them if you want," she said.

Here was another stroke of luck. I quickly began helping her lift down the boxes onto a trestle table. "I've got some other things I must do today," she said. "You can go through these boxes as long as you don't mind the dust."

"I don't mind the dust at all," I responded quickly and immediately took off my suit jacket and rolled up my shirt sleeves. The boxes contained three-by-five cards on which were written each child's name, address, parents' names and some medical information. These were the registration cards from the children's first day at school. Would I be lucky enough to find my daughter's card? I could flip through the boxes quickly, eliminating all the boys, searching for a girl born on Oct. 7, 1952.

After three hours, I was covered in dust and filled with disappointment. I had examined all the boxes and found a half dozen girls born within days of Catherine Anne. However, her registration card was not there. I headed for the men's room, washed off the dust and once again sought out my historian.

"I'm sorry you didn't find what you were looking for," she said. She looked as dejected as I felt. "These children you're looking for, did they finish school? Did they graduate?"

"I don't really know," I answered, "I suppose so."

"Well, I do know that graduation lists exist. You'll have to visit all the high schools but they do have them."

Mentally, I did some quick calculations. If Catherine Anne began school in 1958, she should have graduated in 1970, or a year or two on either side. I would have to make another big assumption: that she had completed her schooling in the county. What if her family had moved? I could be undertaking a lot of time-consuming research without getting any closer to finding her. "Are there no other registration records?" I asked.

"There may be a few in some of the older schools but you've seen most of the ones that survived the fire."

"Then I don't seem to have any choice. I'll have to assume the children I'm looking for finished their schooling here." I had never admitted, in any of our conversations, that I was really looking for only one girl. "Do you have the graduation lists here?"

"No, you will have to go to each school for them."

"Will they let me see them?"

She hesitated before answering, almost as if she was apologizing for what she had to tell me. "It's up to each principal," she finally answered. "Some of them might be a little difficult. They can be quite reluctant about giving out any information concerning a student, without permission." Then she said, "You are on your own. There's nothing more I can do to help you."

I sensed that I inadvertently had walked into a past squabble that had nothing to do with me. I thanked her for all her help and cooperation and left the Board of Education offices. I was disappointed but I had to accept that the school registration records were incomplete and that I had already examined those that still existed. Graduation lists, albeit second best, were my next best source of information. With only one way to find out if I could obtain the lists, I decided to try my luck at one of the nearby Guelph high schools.

I stopped at the John F. Ross Collegiate Vocational Institute. At the office, I asked if they had the list of graduates for the years I sought. The lady in the office told me that the school did not keep such lists. My heart sank. However, she continued, "We still have the registration cards. You can look at those if you wish."

She led me to a room crammed with rows and rows of cabinets. The drawers contained more of those ubiquitous three-by-five filing cards. There seemed to be thousands of them but we soon located the years I was looking for. Once again, I began searching card by card for anyone born on Oct. 7, 1952. This was going to take me forever. Over the years, the cards had become mixed up and, to be certain I did not miss any, I was going to have to go through every drawer in the cabinet. It could take me several days.

Just then, the lady from the office returned and asked, "Would these help?"

She handed me several folded papers which I soon discovered were the printed programs given parents and students at the graduation ceremonies for 1969, 1970 and 1971. Included in each was a list of the graduating students. This was exactly what I needed. I would not have to go through all those drawers after all.

Returning to my car, I assessed what I had learned at the Board of Education office and at this high school, the first of many I would have to visit. I had examined all the school registration cards that had survived the fire of some previous year and none of the girls had been born on Oct. 7, 1952. On the other hand, graduation lists from all the schools might be obtainable. Yet the fundamental weakness in my plan knawed at me. Originally, I had accepted the risk that Catherine Anne had lived in the county long enough to register for school, a period of six years. Now, if I relied on graduation lists, I would have to assume that she continued to live in the county for another twelve years.

Despite the gamble, I could not think of another way to get the information I needed. I decided to continue gathering the graduation lists. There was barely time left in the day to stop at the second of Guelph's four high schools. And this time, I did not meet with the same spirit of cooperation I had enjoyed earlier on. The office was busy with students dashing in and out with their questions and concerns. When I finally got someone's attention, my request was flatly refused by a young woman who adamantly stated, "Student records are confidential." I responded with equal firmness, arguing that high school annuals were public documents and that I had a right to examine them.

My reasoning did not convince her and she stated, "I'll have to check with the principal."

This was exactly what I did not want to happen. The principal could ask me some very awkward questions. I softened my approach and said, "Look, I can see you are very busy. I don't want to cause you a lot of unnecessary work. Why don't I go to the school library and look at the annuals there?"

"Just a minute," she said, walking over to another woman at the other side of the office. They talked for a few minutes, glancing in my direction from time to time. Finally, she went into another room, emerging a few minutes later with the school annuals I had requested. "Here," she stated brusquely. "You can look at them here at the counter but you can't take them away." She returned to her desk a few feet away, obviously to keep her eye on me.

This was hardly an atmosphere in which I could request the use of a photocopier. Fortunately, I had brought paper with me. I stood at that counter for over an hour, copying down the names of all the girls who had graduated from that school during my three-year research period. All the while students were brushing up against me asking questions of the staff or trying to explain why they were late for this or that class. It was very distracting, but I eventually completed my list. Catching the eye of the young lady who had reluctantly provided me with the annuals,I gave her my best smile and gushed thanks for her cooperation. I might need her help again in the future, I told myself. I left the school knowing that I was very lucky. I was not at all sure that I would have survived the principal's questioning, had he actually been summoned. I had succeeded in getting my list but my present method was too risky. I had to have a better story.

7

A Photograph in a School Annual

I spent the evening reviewing what I had learned at the Board of Education offices and the two Guelph high schools. The next day, I would have at least seven schools to visit and I did not have very much time. How could I get willing cooperation? If I told the truth, principals would certainly refuse to give me the graduation lists I needed. The only alternative was to lie. I had been using half-truths for several days, but at first I was bothered by the thought of having to create an outright lie. Then I told myself, if you are going to get the information you require to find your daughter, you must be prepared to lie. It disturbed me to discover how easily I accepted that fact.

Alright, if I must cloak my approach with a falsehood, what should it be? Why would someone like myself be seeking the names of girls who graduated from school eleven years previously? Suddenly, an entirely unrelated event entered my mind and I had the beginning of my story. My father had died recently and he had named me in his will as executor. It was a small and simple estate to deal with but the formalities had occupied me for some weeks. This gave me an idea: suppose a will named me executor of an estate and instructed me to locate a girl whose whereabouts were unknown? I could imply that this girl, if located, would receive an inheritance. And I could hint just enough to suggest that the person I was asking to assist me might also be helping a former student receive an unexpected sum of money.

The question remained of how someone could be named in a will when her actual name was not known. This time I borrowed part of the plot from a book I had once read. I would answer that my father had requested in his will that I try to locate the daughter of an old friend. They had been buddies during the war and had vowed to remember each other's children in their wills. They had lost contact in the years following but now my father left me with this last request.

If pressed, I could go on to explain that I had since learned that my father's friend had died many years before, leaving a wife and very young daughter. The woman had remarried and the girl had taken the name of her stepfather. Because I did not know that man's name I was forced into my present investigation. It was easy to elaborate upon my story. I could add that I had also discovered that they had lived in the area and, I was pretty sure, the girl had attended this school.

To the specific question, "How can a list of girls' names help you?" I could respond that my father had known the birth date of his friend's daughter. Then I would say that I might return at some later date, with a request that a short list of names be checked for birth dates. Finally, I would give an air of urgency to the matter by suggesting that I had limited time and that if my current investigation did not produce results, I would have to use my authority as executor to settle the estate in other ways.

I ran the story over and over in my mind and, far-fetched as it was, decided that it just might work. A refusal to respond to my request for information would make anyone feel very guilty. They would be made to think that they might be responsible for the loss of a former pupil's inheritance if they did not cooperate. On the other hand, any individual would feel gratified if the help he or she offered actually resulted in the girl's identification. The more I thought about it, the more I became convinced that my story would enable me to get the lists I required.

At this point I must try to assuage my conscience. As I have already explained, I had come to terms with resorting to a lie. What follows shows how real people responded to that lie. Should any of them read these words, I hope they will understand.

Looking at my county map, I prepared my route for the next day's efforts. It was going to be a very busy day. In addition to Guelph, there were nine towns I would have to visit. I would start with Clifford, Harriston, Palmerston and Mount Forest to the north. In the afternoon I would go to Arthur, Drayton, Fergus and Elora on my way to Erin at the eastern edge of the county. Guelph presented a problem. When I had asked the lady at the ministry whether Catherine Anne's adopting parents were a Toronto couple, she had replied, "No, they were from a small town." That would appear to eliminate a city the size of Guelph. Yet would a Toronto resident not consider Guelph a small town also, particularly in 1952?

There was another reason I felt I must include Guelph in my search. There was the distinct possibility that the adopting father lived in one of the other towns in the county but practised his profession in the city. Most of the smaller towns were within fairly easy commuting distance. I finally decided to include Guelph even though, for some unknown reason, the other communities seemed more promising to me. I had planned my route for the next day and my story was ready and rehearsed. After a good night's sleep, I awoke eager to embark upon my day's research.

Most people think executors are lawyers but, in fact, they do not have to be. Anyway, I had been mistaken frequently for a lawyer and so, to fit the part, I purposely dressed in my blue pin-striped suit. My first stop was at the Central Wellington District High School in the town of

Fergus. The morning was clear and bright but the radio had predicted clouds for later in the day. There was also a chill in the air that hinted of winter's first snowfall. I found the school easily and, clutching my legal looking briefcase, I walked into the office and asked for the principal's secretary. When she appeared I went into my well-rehearsed story and immediately sensed her interest and understanding. Asking me to wait, she said, "I'll just talk to the principal and see if there's any problem."

It was only a matter of minutes before the principal was standing before me. He expressed his fascination with my tale and promised all the help I required. I felt a twinge of conscience as I followed him into his private office. He instructed his secretary to get the records I sought and have them photocopied for me to take with me. As we waited, he plied me with more questions but none of them gave me any difficulty. The secretary soon returned with the lists I needed. From the moment I entered the school the whole process had taken barely a half hour. Moreover, I had the principal's promise of cooperation should I wish him to check individual records at some later date.

As the weatherman had predicted, it was beginning to cloud over when I left Fergus but I still enjoyed the drive through the rural countryside as I headed for Palmerston. The response at Norwell District Secondary School was again positive as I related my story. This time, however, it was the head counsellor who greeted me. He said that he was willing to help in any way he could. Much to my surprise he produced not only the girls' names I required but their final examination results as well. These, I explained, were not necessary and he agreed to cut them from the photocopies he gave me.

Secure in my briefcase were the complete lists of high school graduates from two of the five schools I wanted to visit on this particular day. I was elated with my success so far as I strolled down the town's main street to a coffee shop. I liked this town — it was quiet and peaceful, a good place for a young girl to grow up. Until now, Palmerston had been unknown to me but I felt comfortable in it.

My visit to the Mount Forest District High School proved that the best of schemes can be derailed by the unexpected. I found the school office in a state of tension and confusion. The secretary said she would be happy to cooperate but she explained that the principal himself was in the midst of a police investigation and that, in fact, the police were in the school at that very moment. This made me a little uneasy, to say the least. There had been a break-in at the school the previous night and whoever it was had tried to open the vault with an explosive, causing more smoke than damage. However, his efforts had made the combination lock on the vault door inoperable — and the records I sought were in that vault.

The secretary said there should be no problem getting the information I was seeking once the vault door was opened, the police were gone and things were back to normal. She promised that she would speak to the principal about my request and mail the material to me at my home. I had no choice but to accept her word. In any case, I did not feel too happy about using my fabricated story in such circumstances.

As it turned out, this school and its cautious principal were to cause me considerable difficulty. I had left my Vancouver address with the secretary but, after waiting several weeks, I did not receive the promised list of names. I wrote the principal repeating my request and included a brief explanation about why I required the list of girls' names. Putting my story in writing made me rather nervous but there did not appear to be any other way to get the information I required. Several more weeks passed before he responded, declining my request on the grounds that such information was confidential.

This was the very thing the lady in the School Board offices had warned me about. She had agreed with me that published school annuals were public documents. I was not asking for school records such as details of courses completed and marks received.

This principal, however, was taking the position that information of any kind about a student was confidential. How was I to persuade him to change his mind?

I decided to go over his head. I appealed to the school superintendent and, in so doing, may have inadvertently closed the door to other adoption searchers in that school district. I was very careful in how I worded my letter to him. I explained that I was "trying to locate a family with long connections to my own." I told him how I had obtained the lists of graduating students from all of the other district schools. His response made things even more difficult for me:

> I was most interested in your request as it is one of literally dozens that we get addressed to our schools for information which we consider to be of a confidential nature. In this day of concerns over confidentiality I am sure you can appreciate our position in matters of this nature.
>
> The principal of Mount Forest District High School was quite correct when he did not release the list of names of graduating students from his school. I am surprised at your statement "I obtained these lists from all but the Mount Forest District High School." I can only assume from that statement that the remaining eight secondary schools did provide you with these lists.
>
> At the present time I am not prepared to request the principal to release this information.

I could just imagine the fuss I had stirred up. No doubt the superintendent had telephoned each of the school principals to check out my claim. Now, anyone else trying to gain access to this information in any of these schools would find it far more difficult. Furthermore, the superintendent had called to task all the principals and secretaries who had been so helpful to me. I had just grown used to lying about my objectives. Now I had to accept as well that I had knowingly used these people, bringing down the wrath of the superintendent on their heads. And as far as my search was concerned, I still lacked the graduation lists from Mount Forest District High School.

Not for the first time since I began my search I was angry at the situation in which I found myself. Because I felt that I had a legitimate right to do so, I was searching for my daughter. Yet, once again, I was having to resort to lies and deceit in my efforts to find her. In addition, it was possible that I was hurting others in the process. My daughter, wherever she might be, her adoptive parents and her natural mother and father were all mature adults, but the law stated that we had no right to find each other. Here I was, lying and cheating to circumvent that law — a law which many professionals in the field had already decided needed to be changed.

Despite my anger and disgust at some of the methods I was using, I was not about to give up now. I had to do something to reassure that school superintendent and quell his concern about what his principals and staff had already done for me. I was going to need a lot more help from these people later, after I had worked over my list of names. I decided to telephone the gentleman and try to persuade him to cooperate with my research efforts.

He turned out to be an extremely friendly and forthright individual who explained to me the difficulty he had with my request. I learned that I was not the first to tread this path. On many occasions in the past he had received requests similar to mine, many of which involved parents looking for their children after custody battles. He gave me a chill when he said he was aware that many people used information obtained from the schools to assist in adoption-reunion searches. There was nothing I could do but keep talking, trying to convince him that my reasons for searching were totally innocent. Much to my relief, I eventually succeeded and he said that he would instruct the principal to send me the list of graduates I needed. Needless to say, I thanked him profusely.

I will probably never know if he actually believed me. He left me with the impression that he felt I was being responsible in what I was doing. The Mount Forest list of graduates arrived about a week later and I remain grateful for the superintendent's intervention, regardless of what he really felt about my request.

The break-in at the school and the presence of the police had shaken my confidence a little but I drove on to the next town, determined to stick to my story. The next school was the smallest of those I would be visiting and the office reflected its size. Even the counter seemed lower, as I crouched down to speak through the hole in the glass partition. On the other side was a woman who had to be the terror of the school — she looked every bit the hard-nosed battle-axe that seems a part of every school staff. Whether she suspected I was a travelling salesman or an angry parent I do not know, but her attitude was anything but friendly.

Having explained my quest to her, she glared at me through her sequin-trimmed glasses. "Well, I'm awfully busy. Can you come back later?"

I explained that I was from Vancouver and had to return the next day.

"Who is going to pay for the photocopy machine?" she inquired.

"Oh, I'll happily pay for that."

"Well then, I guess it's alright. You'll have to wait for me to find the right book."

The right book turned out not to be the high school annual in question but a standard lined notebook, used for keeping track of petty cash. After twenty minutes or so she summoned me once again to the speaking hole in the glass partition and handed the photocopies I wanted along with the petty cash notebook in which was written "12 sheets photocopy @ 5¢ = 60¢." I immediately paid and obediently signed on the dotted line. After this acknowledgment of my use of public property I fled from the office. I could not help wondering what wrath I would have incurred had I not had the right change.

It was now mid-afternoon. The sky was grey and threatening as I headed for the last school on my schedule for the day. By this time, my story was automatic. I was not the least bit surprised when the women in the office at Erin District High School gave my access to the school annuals without any hesitation at all. They did not offer me the use of the photocopier. Instead, they suggested that I sit at a nearby table and make my own list from the annuals. This was going to be a bit of a chore; Erin being one of the larger schools in the district, it took me some time to copy down the names from each page. I had finished with two of the annuals and was about halfway through the last when one girl's picture leapt from the page and stopped me cold.

It was a typical graduation picture with smiling face, makeup perfect and every hair in place. There was nothing special about it at all except that the face I was staring at was the face of my young sister. It was uncanny. The girl in the picture was my sister, when she too posed for her graduation. But it couldn't be. My sister was older and she had never been within miles of this school.

The significance of what I was looking at was obvious. Through the mystery of genes this girl bore a striking resemblance to my sister. They could easily be niece and aunt. This girl had to be Catherine Anne. Someone unrelated could not possibly look so much the same.

The implication was frightening. It was late in the afternoon and I was getting tired. I was actually afraid of the possibility that I had found my daughter. It was too soon. It had been too easy. What should I do now?

I was distracted by a group of laughing students descending on the counter to joke about something with the staff. Everything seemed very happy and normal, bringing me back to a sense of reality. If the girl in the picture was my daughter then that was what I was here for, wasn't it? The only thing to do was to find out more about her.

When the students had gone, I told the young woman who had provided me with the school annuals that I had finished with them. "There is one girl that already fits much of the information I have. I wonder if there's any way you might be able to check her birth date for me?"

I did not get the same eager response that I had received earlier, but she left me to discuss my request with a colleague nearby. As I waited, my mind raced ahead to other ways I might be able to discover the girl's birth date. I had not thought of any when the woman returned and said, "It may be on the records in the other office. I'll just go and take a look."

To help her and perhaps ease her mind I said, "I don't need to know when she was born. All I would like to know is whether she was born on Oct. 7, 1952." This information did seem to end her concern and she disappeared into the back office. I waited by the counter. I was apprehensive but I desperately wanted the birth dates to match. Looking around, I wondered if Catherine Anne had walked down the halls that I could see through the glass wall behind me. Or had she stood right where I was standing now, like any other student seeking the help of the office staff?

I walked over to a large glass case and examined the ribbons and silver cups and shields on display. There had been trophy cases such as this in every school I had visited that day — cups for basketball and softball, a trophy for volleyball. Had Catherine Anne played for any of these teams? Beside the case, pictures of past class presidents gazed down with all the earnestness of their responsibility.

Had she ever been elected to her school council? Perhaps she had been valedictorian of her graduating class.

The woman was coming out of the office and approaching the counter. "I'm sorry," she said, "that's not her birth date."

That was it, nothing more. She had turned and walked back to her desk. I could not believe it. It was like a cold shower — I was so certain that the resemblance could not just be coincidence. I was shattered but there was nothing to do but leave the office. I stuffed the new lists I had made into my briefcase and walked down the corridor, a hallway that just a few minutes before I had imagined echoing with my daughter's laughter.

As I drove back to my hotel, I still could not accept that a girl so closely resembling my own sister could not be related — could not be Catherine Anne. It had started to snow and the countryside was turning a soft white just as dusk was settling. I was surprised at how emotionally exhausted and upset I was. Somehow I knew my daughter had lived in one of the towns I had visited today. I had a strong feeling that I had been very close to her. A couple of times I even thought that I had found her.

8

A Winter's Work

A long telephone conversation with Inge helped restore my sense of perspective. Yet I was still desperately disappointed with my experience at the Erin District High School. To this day, I cannot explain the amazing resemblance between that girl's picture and my young sister — it was one of the most dramatic experiences to occur during my entire search. I felt that I had been looking at a picture of my daughter and, for the first time, she had become real to me.

The next day my story proved effective once again. I did not have any trouble getting the lists I needed from the remaining schools and, indeed, at the last school I thought for a brief moment that I had struck gold. After accepting the usual photocopied sheets, I glanced through them to make sure that they covered the years I had requested. On the second page my eye caught one name and, once again, I felt that eerie feeling. The third name on the page was "Catherine Anne Stewart."

It had never before occurred to me that the adopting parents of my daughter might have kept the name her mother had given her at birth. Was it possible that I was looking for a girl still named Catherine Anne? More important, what about this girl on the list I was now holding? The lady in the office had noticed my hesitation and asked, "Is something wrong?"

"No, not at all," I responded, "it's just that I have noticed one particular girl's name on this list. I've learned from my other investigations, it's possible the name of the young girl I am looking for is Catherine Anne."

The lady had obviously worked at the school for some time because as she looked at the name she said, "Oh, I knew Cathy. She was a lovely girl but I don't know where she is now."

"By any chance would you know her birth date?"

"No, I don't. But I think I could find out in a minute. Can you wait?"

I willingly agreed to wait while she looked for the birth date and settled myself in a chair in the reception area. Surely it would be just too coincidental for this girl to be my daughter.

Ten minutes had passed when she returned and said, "I have it here. Cathy was born on Oct. 23, 1952."

It was close but not close enough. This "Cathy" was not the Catherine Anne I had been seeking. But I had learned to be particularly alert for girls of that name.

Except for Mount Forest, I now had the names of every girl who had graduated from a high school in Wellington County. Even at Mount Forest, the secretary had promised to send the particular list to me within the week. Still, the glaring weakness of my strategy continued to bother me. I was assuming that Catherine Anne had graduated from one of these schools. If so, her name was now in my briefcase. But there was always the chance that her family had moved before she graduated.

Putting that worry aside, I turned to the material I would need to create my second list, which I would use to cross-reference against my list of girls' names. As I had been driving from school to school, I had been doing a lot of thinking about this second project. The lady at the ministry had said that the adopting father was in his early forties and was a professional. What was a professional? I started to make a list of the obvious professions such as doctors, lawyers and dentists. To these I added pharmacists, chiropractors, accountants, architects and teachers. Then I crossed off teachers. Although they might consider themselves members of a profession, I felt the word professional would not normally apply, especially in 1952.

As I was travelling around the vicinity of Guelph, I had come across the School of Veterinary Medicine. At first, veterinarians had not come to my mind as candidates. Yet their training school was an important institution in the area. Surely local residents would class them as professionals? I added them to my list.

I finally decided to make two lists. The first would contain the readily accepted professionals; the second would include schoolteachers, music teachers, university professors and any others I thought of as a collected the material I needed. In the notes I had made following my meeting at the ministry, I had put down my impression that the woman I had spoken with had implied a narrow definition to her use of the word professional. I decided to apply my first efforts to those names associated with such a limited definition.

I drove next to the Guelph Public Library. Libraries are wonderful places — I could not do without them in my work. Once again, I was to bless all those wonderful people who collect papers and records and file them away, just in case someone like me walks in and asks for them. Spending the first hour finding out everything I could about Wellington County and the towns within it, I confirmed that the boundaries had remained the same over the last thirty years. I also collected detailed maps and population counts for all the towns.

One of the librarians helped me locate a "Classified Business Directory" for Guelph, printed in 1952. This was exactly what I needed, and a quick glance made me feel that it was my lucky day. There they were: accountants and auditors, architects, barristers and solicitors, dentists, druggists, music teachers, opticians, optometrists, physicians and surgeons and veterinary surgeons. I decided to omit piano tuners, blacksmiths and horse-shoers. I noted with some curiosity that Guelph boasted three apiarists in 1952, although I didn't think that bee-keeping would likely be classed as a profession.

There were not very many names, four or five dozen at the most. The directory even included their home addresses, which might prove to be helpful later, I thought. For Guelph, at least, I now had lists of most, if not all, the professionals who had worked there at the time of my daughter's adoption. The librarian told me that the smaller towns in the county did not publish business directories in 1952. Since it was essential that I obtain the same sort of list of names for each of the nearby communities, this was a dilemma until I thought about telephone directories. A professional would certainly have a telephone.

I went to the office of the Bell Telephone Company, where I received the disappointing news that they did not have the directories I required. They also told me, however, that their Montreal headquarters maintained a historical section which might be able to help me. Soon after I returned home, my written inquiry to that office produced an immediate response. Yes, they had in their archives the telephone directories for all the communities in Wellington County for the year 1952. They sent me copies and it was then quite easy to identify the names of those I was seeking.

It was time to return to Toronto. The main public library had some of the more detailed records I wanted. There I located the Canadian Law List for 1952, which identified all lawyers practising in Ontario and included the towns and cities where they maintained their offices. This helpful publication even stated the year each lawyer had been called to the bar. Since I knew that the father had been in his early forties at the time of Catherine Anne's adoption, it was easy to calculate those lawyers who would be eligible for my list. They would have had to begin their practice around 1936. If I included a couple years on either side of this, I could compile my list of lawyers.

The Ontario Medical Association published similar information which would prove useful as a check against the names I had already compiled in Guelph. For a time, I thought that the preparation of my list was going to be relatively easy — but I was not to be so lucky with the other professions. Dentists, accountants, pharmacists and architects were not nearly as diligent in publishing membership lists, at least as far as the library was aware. Nevertheless, I was able to obtain the addresses of their professional associations and I later acquired what I needed.

My briefcase was now bulging with hundreds of photocopies, maps and handwritten lists. As there did not appear to be anything more to be achieved on this trip, I decided that it was time for me to return home and make some sense out of all the names I had collected. Besides, I had to get back to work, since my vacation had ended.

I must confess that I was rather pleased with the results of my first efforts as a private detective. I had narrowed my search area to one that seemed to be workable. I had produced a strategy that had a possible chance of identifying the adoptive name of my daughter and where she had attended school. And I had collected the material necessary for me to proceed with my search strategy.

My radio talk show was on the air for three hours, five days a week. There was a tremendous amount of time-consuming preparation involved. Inge and I had to read scores of papers, magazines and books, contact potential guests and prepare interviews. Inge acted as my program producer and by the end of each day we were both quite exhausted. We always looked forward to a relaxing evenig together. Now, however, we had to spend our evenings sorting through all the papers I had brought back home.

Over the next winter, I spent two or three hours every night preparing my two lists for cross-referencing. It was tedious work — a single mistake could undo all my efforts. Any name accidentally missed could be that of my daughter or her adoptive father. In a looseleaf binder, I created a section for each school and entered into it the names of every girl who had graduated from that school between 1969 and 1971. It began to look a little discouraging when the size of these lists grew and grew. But I still hoped they would become manageable when I was able to cross-reference to a list of professionals.

The second list took even longer to assemble. It was time-consuming work to sift through the names of all the doctors and lawyers in practice in 1952. Then I had to pick out those who worked Ontario and, finally, those who lived and worked in Wellington county. I had written letters to the other professional associations and they eventually produced membership lists similar to those I already had. These ones were not nearly so well-organized, and it took several weeks before I had a list of potential candidates for each town. I then entered these names into the appropriate section of my looseleaf.

Bell Canada's historical department had responded to my inquiries by sending me all the 1952 telephone books for the county. My next step was to go through them page by page and highlight every professional name. These names I checked against the lists from the associations. Where I had been able to obtain city directories, I checked these as well for anyone else I had missed. Finally I was satisfied that I had the names of just about every professional who lived or worked in Wellington county at the time of my daughter's birth.

While we were working during these evenings, Inge and I fantasized continuously about Catherine Anne. I suppose it was because the names on our seemingly endless lists were those of real girls, any one of which might be her. By then we had cast aside our frightening worries that something horrible might have happened to her. Crib death, car accident, horrible disease — we had thought about all the possibilities. But none of them seemed possible, now that we had the names of real girls from the region where we knew Catherine Anne had lived.

We wondered what she looked like. Was she tall like most of the girls in my family or shorter like Carol? Was she blonde or brunette, pretty or plain? Did she receive a musical education as her mother had wished? If so, what instrument did she play? Had she been a good student? Had her adoptive parents faithfully gone to parents' night at the local school to hear stories of inattention and incomplete assignments? Who had accompanied her to her graduation dance?

The questions would multiply as we speculated on whether or not she had attended university and, if so, in what faculty. Catherine Anne was now past her thirtieth birthday. Perhaps she was married with her own family to care for. That would mean I was a grandfather. Inge kidded me about it over and over again as we speculated about how many children Catherine Anne might have, as well as their sex and age. Of course, we thought most about where she lived and whether she was happy and content with her life. We also wondered about whether she ever thought about her natural mother and father.

It was time-consuming work and every few days the doubts would surface. We realized that what we were doing might be a complete waste of time. Even if I had found the right area and collected the right lists, I could have missed one name or overlooked an obvious connection. Then the old questions would surface. Should I be looking for my daughter in the first place? Perhaps she was a happy, well-adjusted woman, content in her adoptive family. If I suddenly appeared, I could hurt her deeply. Then I would have to remind myself once more of my original goal. I had to know if Catherine Anne was alive and well.

About this time a rather severe health problem intervened. I had been finding normal breathing becoming more and more difficult — the slightest exercise, such as climbing a flight of stairs, left me gasping for breath. Specialists were consulted and they concluded that I was suffering from allergic asthma. I had horrible visions of an emphysema ward. Then a specialist in respiratory medicine predicted that, if I stopped smoking and got more exercise, I could overcome my condition with the aid of minor medication.

Hay fever or sinus allergies had been something I had grown to live with for over twenty years. The doctor explained to me that there was something in my genetic make-up that had caused these reactions to move to my lungs. My fight to rid myself of the nicotine habit is another dramatic story, but I succeeded in quitting smoking and my health improved dramatically. A surgeon corrected what my genes and lifestyle had done to my nose and I received a new lease on life. Yet this abrupt reminder of human fragility, combined with a radio interview I conducted at about the same time, caused me to think very seriously about an aspect of adoption I had not yet considered.

Realizing that much of my own medical problem had a genetic origin, I began to wonder whether my daughter carried these same genes. Might she suffer from the same allergic reactions? I knew already that many of my symptoms were shared by others in my family. Why would it stop with me? Because of her adoption, Catherine Anne would never know the significance of the genes she carried within her. Furthermore, she may have already passed them on to her children.

One day, I had a guest on my program who was the doctor in charge of the genetic screening program in Vancouver's largest maternity hospital. I asked her to give my listeners an example of how modern genetic screening techniques had helped doctors in their diagnosis and treatment. Much to my surprise, her answer concerned an adopted child. Her story was more significant to me than she could have ever imagined.

She related how geneticists had identified a family as being carriers of myotonic dystrophy, a disease that involves wasting of muscles and loss of coordination, formation of cataracts in the eyes and mental retardation or a gradual loss of mental acuity. The first child born to the woman in this family had died at the age of three months. Two years later, the same woman gave birth to another child. She also showed symptoms of the disease.

A thorough genetic screening traced the disease back through several generations in the mother's family. Her father showed symptoms as did her sister and aunt. Further investigation identified myotonic dystrophy in the great-grandmother and great-great-grandmother. The doctors told the mother that an amniocentesis test would, in all probability, show whether any future fetus carried the disease. Despite this, two years later this same woman gave birth to another baby with congenital myotonic dystrophy.

Again the doctors urged the entire family to submit to genetic counselling. It was only then that the mother revealed that she had borne yet another child, seven years before, which she had given up for adoption. She was unsure whether the father was her present husband or another man with whom she was having an affair at the time. The counsellor was aware for the first time that, somewhere, there was a seven-year-old girl who had a fifty per cent risk of developing this disease. Furthermore, she could go on to produce a family of her own, completely unaware of the defective gene she might pass on to her children.

As it happened in this particular case, the court agreed with the counsellor's concern and granted access to the adoption records of the child. This enabled the couple to make contact with the adoptive parents. The information they received about their little girl was frightening and upsetting, but they agreed to have her seen by specialists. The girl's genetic history, with all its implications, was now critically important to her adoptive parents and their medical advisors. Her family doctor would not normally have suspected myotonic dystrophy as the cause of any medical problems this youngster might experience in the future. Knowledge of her genetic past would now make possible appropriate treatment.

My guest went on to explain that, in at least thirty percent of the adoptions referred to her department, genetic background information is included with the babies' medical records and is discussed with adopting parents. This percentage is increasing rapidly with the dramatic increase in knowledge about genetics, particularly as new tests are perfected which pinpoint specific genes with total accuracy.

Inevitably, I connected this story with what I had recently learned about my own genetically related medical problems. I wondered if Catherine Anne had ever required genetic information about her natural family that was denied to her because she was adopted. My search efforts gained new motivation.

It was the summer of the following year before Inge and I were finally able to begin the all-important cross-referencing between the two lists we had now completed for Guelph and all the other towns in Wellington County. Only now would we see exactly how many girls' names would be on our short lists and how big a task it would be to check each birth date. For each town and each school, I compared the surnames of the professionals against the surnames of the school graduates. I made a separate list of those names that matched. As we worked, I could not help thinking that Catherine Anne's birthday was approaching. She would be thirty years old in a matter of weeks. After all the hours we had spent on these lists, would they help us find her?

As I had hoped, what finally emerged were short lists ranging form six to a dozen names for each of the smaller schools. The four Guelph schools produced longer lists but even they did not exceed twenty names each. I wrote letters to all the high school principals reminding them of my visit the previous year. I asked them to check the birth dates of the girls on an enclosed list. Once again, I did not ask them to reveal the actual birth dates but only to inform me if any of the girls were born on Oct. 7, 1952. This accomplished, there was nothing to do but wait for their replies.

I knew that it was a long shot. Apart from the fact that I had missed the names of any girls whose families had moved from the county since the adoption, I could never be sure exactly what the ministry official meant when she told me that the man who adopted my daughter was a professional. All I could do was hope that I was going to be lucky.

9

Sharing the Secret

The letters to all the school principals were in the mail. Since I knew it would be several weeks before I could expect any replies, Inge and I decided to take a vacation. It occurred to me that an airplane accident or something similar could result in our deaths, leaving behind the results of all our investigations. My sons were named as my executors and they would discover this material, which would possibly contain the actual name of my daughter. It was time to tell them about their sister.

We discussed the best way to break the news to them about my wayward youth and its result, and the efforts we had already made to find their sister. A family dinner seemed the appropriate setting, and so we invited the three of them and their wives to join us that weekend. We met together as a family frequently, but the nature of our dinner invitation had apparently tipped them to the fact that something special was up. Months later, they told us that they had conferred before coming to the house, trying to guess what had happened to warrant such a family conference. Needless to say, none had guessed the true reason for our meeting.

We have all laughed about that dinner together many times since. They had all arrived in a gloomy mood because the consensus was that something serious had happened between Inge and me. They thought that we were going to announce our separation, or worse, an intended divorce. Looking back, we had been preoccupied with our discovery and search and, over the last few months, had given them the accurate impression that something very serious was on our minds. In any case, none of them asked any questions, waiting instead for me to explain the reason that I wanted us all together that particular weekend. I now realize that a sense of drama hung rather heavily in the air.

After dinner, we all moved into the living room. I ended the suspense by telling them exactly what had occurred. Their first reaction to my revelation was a stunned silence. Then the questions began and, before long, they had the full story. There was even an attempt at humour as my oldest son suggested that he always suspected I was a "dirty old man."

It was clear, however, that these young men were having some difficulty accepting the existence of a sister, albeit a half-sister. They had grown up in a very male environment. Suddenly to acknowledge a sister was difficult enough, but an *older* sister — that was going to take some time. Their wives, on the other hand, seemed to relate to the situation far more easily. Their questions and comments were sensitive and understanding.

If I was expecting them all to react with the same excitement and enthusiasm that I now felt about my daughter I was to be disappointed. It was as if my sons were saying, "This is your business, Dad. It has nothing to do with us." I now realize that they needed some time to let the significance of what I had told them sink in. It is not every day that you learn you have a half-sister whom you have never heard about, and an illegitimate one besides. They also had to get used to the fact that I was searching for her and might actually find her. What would that mean and how would it effect our family circle?

We also told our news to several of our close friends. For one thing, just talking about Catherine Anne helped. We were happy to discover that our friends were not only understanding but supportive in our determination to find my daughter. Most of them became intimately involved in the search, offering comments and suggestions as we progressed. Every time we met, they would ask us for the latest developments. Newcomers to our group would ask me to explain my story from the beginning. I would willingly respond, naively believing in the uniqueness of my situation. This was when I first became aware of how so many others had a similar experience, usually kept a dark secret from relatives and friends.

On one occasion we attended an informal party in the home of one of our friends and the hostess asked me to bring her and her guests up to date about any progress we had made with our search. An hour or so later, one of the women asked me if we could talk privately. It being a lovely warm summer evening, we left the gathering and walked along one of the nearby paths beside the river. She hesitated at first but eventually told me about her pregnancy years before and her decision to give up her baby for adoption. She confessed that she had never forgotten her child and that hardly a day passed without her wondering where she was and whether she needed her. She had spent hours wondering what her daughter had been like as a young child, as a teenager, as a young woman. Was she married now? Did she have children of her own? Was she well? Was she alive?

Because I had not had any reason to think much about adoption before, I had not realized how many women carry such a secret with them. Meeting them was now to become a common occurrence. I would learn intimately about the need to share, the need to seek reassurance, the need to find out the answers to so many questions. Obviously, far more women face this dilemma than do men. The lucky ones have an understanding husband. They can discuss their guilt and their longing to put an end to all the questions. Others confide in a close female friend, frequently one who also gave up a child for adoption. I met few men in my position.

Upon hearing my story, many women confided their secret to me, seeking suggestions about how they too might be able to learn what had happened to their child. There was little I could say other than to tell them what I was doing or to direct them to one of the self-help groups such as Parent Finders. One thing became absolutely clear to me: no matter what the nurses or social workers say at the time, a mother who gives up her baby for adoption never forgets. I was beginning to learn of the inadequacy, indeed the cruelty, of our adoption procedures.

I also learned of the shame. One evening we attended a small dinner party hosted by another friend who had known for some time of my search. There were two other couples at the table, both of whom we had met just that evening. "Barrie, how's the search going?" inquired our hostess. Then, realizing the others at the table were unaware of my story, she asked me to start at the point where Carol first shared her secret with me.

With my background as a radio show host, storytelling comes quite naturally to me. I had already discovered the dramatic effect of my tale — it was good for at least fifteen minutes of table conversation, so I did what my hostess had requested. However, I was not more than a couple of minutes into my account when I became increasingly aware of a growing uneasiness on the part of the woman sitting opposite me. She had stopped eating, her hands in her lap, her eyes glued to some meaningless spot on her dinner plate. I pretended not to notice and rushed through my report on the progress made in my search, whereupon I pointedly changed the topic of conversation.

My puzzled hostess accepted my abrupt diversion of our table talk and the horrible moment passed. But by then, I had ruined the woman's evening by my reminding her of long-buried thoughts and events. I could not help glancing at her husband. Unless he was a fine actor, he was oblivious to the drama that had taken place at the table. Perhaps he was also unaware of any reason why my story would upset his wife. I was certainly aware — I had no doubt whatever that, inadvertantly, I had transported my dinner partner back many years to when she had given up a child for adoption. She had sad memories of the shame of pregnancy and anonymous labour in some unfamiliar hospital or clinic.

As a result of such episodes, Inge and I became very sensitive to the reactions of people hearing our story. Our close friends knew us well and they had long ago formed opinions of our values and character. An illegitimate child in the background was not going to change those opinions. Still, I learned about the strong and emotional feelings many people have concerning adoption, including some outspoken and adamant opposition to my search.

Invariably, this was preceeded by words of understanding for the dilemma in which Carol found herself. "She was right," they would say. "Giving the child up for adoption was the proper thing to do under the circumstances." Then they would go on, "You can only cause damage by what you're doing," or "You have no right to interfere at this stage in your daughter's life." I learned that these comments frequently came from parents who had adopted children themselves.

Such remarks reveal a deep apprehension. To put it bluntly, it is the fear of adoptive parents that a natural mother or father will come along and steal the affection of the child they have nursed and nurtured. Sadly, the institution of adoption itself creates this fear. It does so despite the good intentions of all those involved. Because of imposed secrecy and false birth certificates, all of which is sanctioned and approved by social workers and governments, it is no wonder adoptive parents come to believe that there is a need for it all. I never argued with these people. Trying to reassure them was not appropriate to a social occasion.

One reaction that I found more encouraging and hopeful was acknowledgment that times had indeed changed.

Subjects like premarital sex, pregnancy out of wedlock, and adoption are now acceptable topics for social discussion. I found widespread agreement that perhaps the laws concerning adoption should be reconsidered. There was an admission that there must be a reason for the number of children seeking their natural parents and the number of mothers wanting to know what had happened to their babies.

It is still remarkable to me how adoption touches so many people. I had not expected this at all when I first became personally involved in the subject. When I initially sought legal advice about my situation, my lawyer remarked that he had an adopted child. He told me that he had often wondered if she would, one day, choose to search for her natural parents. Even in a small group, whether the occasions were business or social, I frequently found people present who admitted to an adoption in their family. They may have been adopted themselves, be parents or grandparents of adopted children, or be related in some other way to an adopted child. Meeting all of these people convinced me that I had entered upon a subject that would take me far beyond the specific search for my daughter.

In the meantime, replies to my letters to the Wellington County schools began to arrive. The first few simply stated that none of the girls' birth dates matched that of Catherine Anne. One principal reported a Catherine Mary on my list had a birth date of Oct. 8, 1952, one day away. I later had inquiries made about her just in case, but discovered that she had an older sister. Again, close but not Catherine Anne — just another disappointment.

Another response took me back to one of the Guelph high schools. I well remembered the kind woman in the office who was so helpful. It was she who came up with the graduation day programs containing the lists of all the graduating students. This had saved me the daunting task of examining thousands of three-by-five registration cards. Upon receiving my letter, the principal had given this same woman the task of dealing with my request to check the birth dates. She replied to my correspondence with the information that, again, none of the girls had the right birth date.

It was her note at the end of the letter that reminded me how very careful I had to be in my inquiries. The last thing I wanted to do was to suddenly reveal my identity to my daughter. I wanted to avoid this at all costs. She had written, "I certainly was surprised to see my own name on your list." Who ever would have thought one of the girls I was checking would be working in the school office. While I was certain that I wanted to find my daughter, I had no intention, as yet, of making any personal contact with her, certainly not in such a manner.

Each reply added to our disappointment. Finally, there was only one school left to be heard from. I waited two more weeks and then sent a letter of reminder. The following days were some of my most anxious, for this school represented my last hope. If the answer was the same as the others, my system had failed. All my efforts to date would have been in vain. I would be back where I had started.

Finally, the response arrived. I tore open the envelope to read the one line reply: "I'm sorry but none of the girls on your list was born on the date you mentioned."

I knew my research method had been faulty but I was counting on my luck and it had failed me. Over a year's work had proven to be worthless. The disappointment was overwhelming and, as a result, I shelved the entire search for several weeks. I avoided the subject with friends and did everything I could to wipe the whole thing from my mind. It was Inge who finally ended the gloom. One evening she said, "There's got to be other things we can do. We've got to start all again."

From the work I had already done, I realized the flaws in my search and that was where I had to begin. My list of professionals was simply guesswork. I would have to expand it to include all those others I had earlier placed on my doubtful list. All the schoolteachers I had decided not to include earlier would now be a real challenge to identify. Would their associations have the names of teachers in the county at that time, and would they give them to me? What about bankers, are they professionals? My father had been a bank manager but I do not think he would ever have classed himself as a professional. What about a police officer, is he a professional? A church home for unwed mothers had arranged the adoption. What about church ministers, are they professionals?

If anything, I became more discouraged. I realized that my original assumptions about the man who adopted my daughter were quite arbitrary. The definition of the word professional could be as broad as one wanted it to be. It still made sense to continue with my search along these lines, but I could not help thinking that there might be a better way.

The topic on my radio talk show one day was the expanding use of credit cards and computerized banking. My guests were emphasizing the need for new protective legislation against the unauthorized use of computer records. They claimed that computer records could be transferred from one company to another without the individual's knowledge or permission. Furthermore, they told stories of so-called computer hackers. These were people who obtained confidential information about anyone whose records were in any particular data bank.

By the time the program ended my mind was buzzing with possibilities. Could I find my daughter through computer records? That night, I made a list of the data banks that might contain information about her. My first surprise was to discover just how many such data banks would, in theory, have the information I required. They ranged all the way from Revenue Canada to health insurance carriers. The list seemed unending. Visa and Mastercard, all the gasoline companies and the countless department stores all maintained computerized files on their customers.

From my own experience, I knew there was one absolutely vital piece of information included in every one of these files. That was the birth date. Every credit card application form I had ever completed required me to put down my birth date. This was the one piece of information about Catherine Anne that I knew was factual — I knew her birth date. The possibilities were obvious: if I could find a way to access a data bank, I could ask it to give me a list of everyone born on her birth date.

With such a list, I would have another valuable cross reference with the other information I had already collected. But wait a minute, I told myself — chances are my daughter had married and taken her husband's name. This was a problem but I put it aside for the time being. Obviously, I had to find out more about computers and how to access data banks.

At Simon Fraser University, I met with one of the chief instructors. He gave me a crash course in computers and data banks. I was quite frank with him about my intentions. "You might be able to do it," he said, "but it will be dangerous." He warned me about entry codes and protective devices installed in the larger data banks. "Furthermore," he added, "you might very well face charges under the Criminal Code if you are caught." This poured a large quantity of cold water on my plans.

He told me about computer hackers and the pranks of some of his students who looked at entry codes as nothing more than a challenge. It did not take me long to meet some of them and a couple said that they might help me, should I decide to try to access one of the data banks. However, I wasn't ready for that yet. I didn't even know what data bank to select.

They told me that one of the more sophisticated computer systems was that used by the police. I could hardly go into a police station and ask for their help in what I was contemplating. But I did know a senior police officer well enough to seek his advice. Not surprisingly, he cautioned me against doing anything illegal. On the other hand, he suggested that there was no reason I could not request information from the owners of a data bank. "I doubt it," he said, "but they might be prepared to help." Of far greater assistance was the information he gave me about drivers' licence records.

In every province, drivers' licences are available only to applicants over a certain age. In addition, certain restrictions usually apply when a driver reaches an older age. As a result, the birth date becomes a permanent and significant part of a driver's record. As well, that record is fed into a computer. Every police officer has access, via the national computer network, to the driving record of every driver in every province.

Another police officer in the traffic division confirmed this when I later asked him if he could help me. "I could do it for you," he said. "I'd simply have to ask for the name of every driver in Ontario with that birth date. However, I'm not going to do it," he continued. "There would be too many questions and my neck would be on the line." I could only agree.

The possibilities were so tempting that I put my other research aside and concentrated on those driver's licence records. Again, I would have to make assumptions. I would have to presume that Catherine Anne had a driver's licence and that she had received it in Ontario. Furthermore, she would have had to apply for her licence while she was still using her maiden name. Even if she had married and changed her name, her file would still show her driving record back to the day she first received her licence. It must also include her maiden name. These were fairly safe assumptions. It was worth a try anyway, and I decided to approach the matter directly.

I contacted a senior official I knew in the British Columbia motor vehicle office. He informed me that the office frequently received requests from people seeking lost relatives or, more frequently, lost debtors. The latter were out of luck but the department did what it could to help the others, once having established the legitimacy of their purpose. My problem was that a government agency such as a motor vehicle department would not consider my particular motivation and purpose to be legitimate.

I carefully worded a letter to the Ontario Ministry of Transport and Communications, the agency responsible for drivers' licences in that province. I requested their help in locating a lost relative. After all, this was, strictly speaking, the truth. For obvious reasons, I neglected to mention that the lost relative was an adopted daughter, whom the laws of that same province said I was not to identify, let alone meet. I did not expect too much help from the department officials but, much to my surprise, the reply I received was quite encouraging.

Yes, the department did receive such requests as mine and, within certain limitations, they did provide assistance. I wrote back stating: "For some time, I have been working, almost as a hobby on locating various members of our family who, over the years, have lost touch with each other. I have had a variety of success." This was a true statement, as far as it went. The tracing of our family tree had been a hobby of mine for some years. Indeed, on the face of it, the entire letter was the truth as I continued: "One search has been particularly frustrating. I have been attempting to locate a woman who was born on Oct. 7, 1952 in Toronto. I have a lot of other information about her, but my major problem is I do not know her name."

I went on to ask if it would be possible for them to provide me with a list of all females in possession of a driver's licence who were born on that date. Obviously, it was what my letter did not say that made it a deception.

This time, their response was even more heartening. The writer informed me: "To get an idea of the number of records involved, I had our file traced as part of the regular production run and it turns out that we have 284 women on the file who were born on that date. To locate and print out their total records, would require two passes of the file at a cost between 300 to 400 dollars."

This was the most encouraging news I had received since leaving Guelph, now almost two years ago. I could investigate 284 names relatively easily.

Unfortunately, the letter went on to request further information about the purpose of my search. Particularly, they wished to know more details about the party I was seeking. This was exactly what I could not provide. I was close to a vital piece to my puzzle but how could I provide the information they were seeking?

I had used a fabricated story to get by suspicious school principals. What made me hesitate to do the same thing now? I have never been able to answer that question satisfactorily. Perhaps it was fear of being found out. But even if I had been discovered, I doubt that there would have been very severe consequences. After all, what were the penalties for lying to a public official? In any case, despite the importance of the information I might have obtained and how it would have aided my research, I decided to abandon the idea.

This was the nearest I ever came to gaining access to computer data banks. The more I investigated the possibilities, the more convinced I became that any success in this direction would require a skill and sophistication I did not have. I'm not saying that it isn't possible. Had events not unfolded as they did, I would have persisted but, for the layman, this is a very difficult area. It soon became clear to me there are a lot of people smarter than me designing systems to prevent the very access I was considering.

I next approached the Ombudsman's Office in Ontario. I knew full well that he could intervene only if a government ministry had dealt with me unfairly. I told him how I had never been consulted about the decision to give up my daughter for adoption. I argued it was therefore unfair for the Ministry of Community and Social Services to restrict the information provided me to that normally released to the mother, who had consented to the adoption in the first place.

I was not very hopeful that this letter would accomplish very much. It was a long shot, to say the least. Therefore, it was no surprise when the ombudsman replied stating that he did not accept my argument. He went on to explain the current laws governing adoption in the province and how the courts were interpreting them. He also listed the various government agencies and departments that dealt with adoption matters. I would have saved a lot of time and effort if I had contacted this office at the start of my search. I had spent several weeks acquiring this same information from the university law library. In addition, I had had to pay my lawyer for his time. The fact remained, however, that the ombudsman was not going to help me find my daughter.

There was a paradox in this same letter that I found rather amusing. The ombudsman is not above the law in any sense. And the law in the province not only prohibited access to adoption records, it actively discouraged any reunion, unless all parties to the adoption agreed. Yet the ombudsman's letter encouraged me to contact Parent Finders, an association whose aim is to help people attempting adoption reunion by fair means or foul. Clearly, even in government circles there are conflicting views about adoption laws.

Another winter had passed and I was no further ahead in my search. I could not inspire myself to start all over again on those lists. Yet Catherine Anne would soon be thirty-one. I wondered if her birthday would not be a day on which she might think about her natural parents. If she was curious about us at all, surely on this day she would wonder if her parents ever thought about her. This thought led me in another direction entirely in my search for my daughter.

10

"I Think We've Found Her"

Birth dates are seldom secret. Friends and relations acknowledge them every year. This had to be true for Catherine Anne as well. When I am reading books or the newspapers, I always note with interest others who share my birthday. In the early days of my search I had met several women who had placed advertisements in the newspapers on the birth date of the child they had given up for adoption. What if I placed a notice in all the Ontario newspapers on the day my daughter celebrated her birthday? Perhaps she or a friend would notice it. This might be a method of making contact with her.

Such classified ads had appeared in our local papers. I had also seen several reports in the adoption group newsletters of natural parents making contact with their children by such a method. What I had in mind was a much larger notice than the advertisements I had seen, one that would be attention-grabbing. I had no idea of the costs involved nor what the actual wording of such an advertisement should be. I therefore sought the advice of a friend in the advertising business. He agreed to devise such a campaign and find out the cost. The latter would determine whether I would proceed with the plan.

In the meantime, this same friend suggested that I talk with his wife, a practising lawyer in the city who had dealt with adoption matters in the past. Perhaps she would have some ideas about what steps I might next take in my search. As I was always open to advice and suggestions, I later met with her and it was she who recommended the hiring of a private detective. She said that there were firms that specialized in finding people and there was no reason why their expertise would not equip them for a search such as mine. At first I had my doubts. In the course of my business, I had interviewed several private detectives, but it was usually in connection with a rather unsavory divorce story or a suspected insurance fraud. I had never before thought of hiring such a person, if only because in the movies at least, they always seemed to charge enormous fees. But my friend's wife was so positive about the results I would achieve that I shelved my advertising plan for the time being. Instead, I asked her to contact a detective for me.

A Toronto detective agreed to take my case. The arrangement made with him was that the lawyer would act as intermediary. She would pay his fees from a fund of $5,000 I provided as a start, and the detective would submit regular reports. The first thing I did was give the detective all the information I had gathered to date about Catherine Anne. He said this was not the first adoption case he had undertaken and he was very confident that he would be successful.

Unless you have had cause to hire a detective for such a purpose, you cannot imagine the suspense that follows immediately after he has taken the case. I waited anxiously for each report. I allowed myself to fall into a state of euphoria, anticipating early success. He was a professional, I told myself, and thus it would only be a matter of time before he found Catherine Anne.

The first report I received was humbling, to say the least. It was clear that this private detective did not appreciate an amateur bumbling through his territory. He let me know, in no uncertain terms, that my earlier investigations were making things very difficult for him. He didn't say it outright but he implied that, had I not made these approaches, he would have had far more success. He reported that because of my previous approach someone had flagged the files at both the Minister of Community and Social Services and the Motor Vehicle Branch. As a result, officials there became very suspicious of his inquiries. I had no way of disputing this. On the other hand, I did not believe that any of the people I had spoken to would have revealed any more to him than they had to me.

It was not long before I learned what was really behind the detective's complaint. He felt that my earlier activities had closed the door on one of his investigative techniques. He had been planning to bribe someone, presumably a public servant, to examine the files. Apparently no one was now prepared to take the risk. When I learned this it produced another of my tests of conscience. Despite the obvious temptation, Inge and I decided against authorizing any attempt to use bribery to get the information we were after. Aside from anything else, bribing a public servant is a serious criminal offence with severe consequences for the person caught.

Actually, it was rather flattering to realize that his investigation was beginning in the same places I had already visited. Indeed, as his efforts continued, I became more and more convinced that my amateur sleuthing had not been too far off base at all. What he did provide, however, was manpower and time. I soon began to receive the results of investigations I had earlier contemplated but never had the time to undertake.

He searched the Guelph area newspapers for a possible birth or adoption announcement but without result. Likewise, there was nothing helpful found in the birth records of the Gynecological Society. It was when he checked the Guelph City Birth Registry, something I never knew existed, that the first hopeful development occurred. One of the children in the registry matched the birth date.

When the detective reported this to me, I once again believed that my search might be ending. Each day, I was filled with hope as I waited for the next report. I felt the money I was spending for his services was worth it and I was sure the decision to retain him had been a wise one. However, eight frustrating weeks passed before I received his next report.

The girl the detective had found in the registry, while she had the same birth date, was not adopted. She had several brothers and sisters, both older and younger, and her father was an electrician. It was a false lead, the first of many, and it produced the usual disappointment and discouragement. I simply instructed the detective to carry on with the investigation and continued to await his reports.

I don't know how but, a few weeks later, he was able to locate the doctor who had attended Carol at the Presbyterian Home and delivered her baby. She had retired many years before and had disposed of her patient records long ago. She said that she remembered Carol but could not recall ever meeting the adopting parents. I was impressed that the detective had been able to find her even though she wasn't able to provide any helpful information.

Earlier, I had suggested to the detective the significance of Carol's stay in a home for unwed mothers run by the Presbyterian Church. My personal knowledge of such church agencies was that they would make every effort to see that the child went to a church home, if possible a Presbyterian home. He agreed and said he would try to examine the baptismal records of the Protestant churches in the area, particularly those of that denomination. His report back to me was negative. However, I later realized that he did not carry out this particular assignment very thoroughly.

The detective also agreed with my conclusion that the school records of the area might contain the clue to success.

With several helpers, he returned to the Board of Education offices and spent several days examining much of the same material I had already seen. I was never able to determine exactly what records he inspected or what story he used to gain access to them. I felt this second effort worthwhile since I could very easily have missed a critical name.

Again, several weeks passed before we heard from him. This time, there was no doubt in his report as he stated, "I think we've found her." The hope and excitement caused by those words is hard to describe. Three years had passed since I had learned of Catherine Anne's existence. Now I was going to find out the answers to so many questions. If the detective was correct, I already had an answer to the most important question. My daughter was alive. At this stage, that was all he could tell me.

The next few days passed more slowly than any I could remember as I waited for more details of his discovery. Eventually, the detective reported that the girl in question met all the criteria with one exception. He was unable, as yet, to verify her adoption. His report was particularly fascinating because he disclosed that she was living in some kind of commune on Manitoulin Island at the top of Lake Huron.

"Two things must be done," he said. "We should check out the adoption question and, if you agree, I should go and talk to her."

I immediately authorized further investigation into the question of her adoption. However, I said that I wanted to think carefully about making any direct contact with her. He said that he had a policeman friend in the area who would act for him, in an unofficial capacity, of course. All of a sudden I was looking at the end of my long search. But what I faced was the question I had never, up to then, tried to answer. Now that I had found my daughter, what should I do?

This made me think about the dilemma facing all adopted children who seek their natural parents and such parents, like me, who look for their lost children. At some stage, they must decide, if the search is successful, whether or not to make direct contact. Because our adoption laws fail to provide for the proper exchange of information between the various parties to an adoption, the searcher is unaware of vital factors critical to any responsible answer to this question.

These factors vary depending on whether the searcher is the child or the parent. For example, a child starting a search would obviously know of his adoption. Likewise, the child would know its natural mother was aware of the adoption. Whether or not the natural father or any other members of the family shared this knowledge is one of the unknown factors. If the natural mother has married, the child does not know if the husband is aware of his wife having given up a child for adoption. Matters become even more sensitive if there are other children in the family.

When a parent is searching, there are additional unknown questions. In my own case, I considered each of these questions very carefully. Was my daughter aware that she was an adopted child? Had her parents told her anything at all about her past? Did she have any brothers or sisters, adopted or not, and did they know?

Even more perplexing were the more subjective questions which were equally important in the decision I had to make. If my daughter knew of her adoption, did she have any desire to meet her natural parents? Would the sudden appearance of a natural father and mother disrupt or harm the family relationships which she had developed over the past thirty-two years? In particular, what would be the effect on the man and woman who had devoted a good part of their lives to raising my daughter? How would my actions affect other members of the family group, about whom I knew absolutely nothing?

Most important of all, what would be my daughter's reaction to my abrupt intrusion into her life? If she didn't want anything to do with me or her natural mother she could resent my actions. She might be so angry and upset that I would lose any chance of communication with her in the future. The thought of such an end to my search was painful. Still, she would be able to learn about her blood relatives and their history, should she so choose.

No single question, during the entire period of our search, occupied the thoughts of Inge and me more. But no matter what we said, I always returned to my initial reaction when I first learned of Catherine Anne's existence. I had to know if she was alive and well. Perhaps I could instruct the detective to make contact with the girl on Manitoulin Island and still keep within the bounds of that first goal. Obviously, she was alive. The only question remaining was whether or not she was well.

This latter question now forced me to examine exactly what I meant by well. She could be healthy but desperately unhappy. She could be in serious trouble. What kind of commune was this she was living in? Why was she there? Did she need or want help of any kind, and if so, was I capable of providing it?

I finally had to admit that I was kidding myself. I was not going to be satisfied until I knew whether or not this girl was my daughter. Second, I wanted her to know of my existence and my search for her. If, after that, she didn't want anything to do with me, I would simply have to accept such a decision. As to all the other questions I had tried to take into consideration, I reasoned that this girl was now over thirty years of age and an adult. Surely she was capable of handling my sudden appearance.

Another important factor in my decision was something that had been building up in my mind as I had got deeper and deeper into my search. All adopted children — not just my daughter — were denied knowledge about them- selves and their natural background. The law never took into the account the feelings or desires of these children. I was becoming more and more convinced that an adopted child should have an automatic right to all available information about himself. This should be available regardless of the wishes of any of the parents, natural or otherwise.

I felt a strong obligation to make it possible for my daughter to decide whether she wished to journey down the avenues open to her. I felt that, having come this far, unless I made myself known to her I would be just like everyone else who had denied her access to her natural heritage. I came to the conclusion that any parent of such a child had a responsibility to make all family background information available.

Now that I had decided to devise some means of contact, I examined the alternatives. I thought it rather insensitive for a detective to be the person to tell my daughter that her father was trying to find her; indeed, I felt it would be most inconsiderate to allow any stranger to make such an approach. I finally resolved to locate a close friend or an advisor to my daughter. Perhaps someone like a church minister would agree to act as an intermediary.

Such a person could be open and frank and inform her that her natural parents were anxious to know that she was alright. Should she require help or assistance, he could tell her that her parents would provide it, if they could. Furthermore, he could invite her to communicate with us should she wish. On the other hand, he could make it clear that a rejection by her of any such contact would be respected by me and by her mother. I was not quite sure how I was going to find someone who would act for me in approaching this girl.

There was still no further word from the detective and waiting for more news was becoming unbearable. Meanwhile, I could not resist speculating about the significance of this girl living in a commune. Did it mean she was a member of some sort of cult, like those occupying the headlines at the moment? There were countless stories in the news of young men and women suddenly leaving school or university to don saffron robes and join the band of a travelling guru.

Because she was living in a commune, did that mean she had never married? Perhaps she was divorced. It appeared likely that she did not have any children, which meant I would not suddenly have to accept the role of instant grandfather. Each day brought new possibilities to mind as we awaited further word.

When the detective finally contacted me again he said he was still sure that his investigation had been successful. However, he was having difficulty verifying the adoption. A few days later, he said that he was no longer sure about the adoption after all. In view of this doubt, I told him that no one was to make any contact with the girl.

Detectives, like everyone else, are human I suppose. After building up my hopes, he did not want to admit that he had been wrong. Again, it was several weeks before we heard anything further. This time we expected the news, even if we had retained some tiny hope. He had assumed that there could not possibly be two girls the same age, with the same birth date, and from the same area. Other factors in the girl's background had convinced him that the girl in the island commune must be the one he was seeking. He had raised our hopes too soon. His further investigations, he admitted, showed clearly that the girl was not adopted.

My dreams came crashing to the ground. Inge was equally discouraged and we just couldn't talk about it for several days. The detective's final report arrived and he had no further practical suggestions. He proposed following other avenues but I did not think that any of them held much hope for success. Frankly, I had become rather disillusioned with his methods. His handling of the investigation into the girl on the island had bordered on the reckless.

Our friends shared our gloom, as they too had anticipated an end to our long search. No one seemed to have any further suggestions. Another birthday had come and gone. Catherine Anne was now thirty-two and I was no closer to finding her. One day I said to Inge that I felt we had allowed our search to occupy too much of our time and thoughts. We should give it a rest. I simply did not want to think about it for a while.

I sent word to the detective that I did not wish him to make further inquiries. I put all my files and records away. For almost five months, I made no attempt to proceed with any kind of search. From time to time, Inge and I would discuss what had happened. We shared our disappointment but we lacked the inspiration to try again. Our friends learned not to ask about it, knowing how frustrated we had become and how helpless we felt. "Perhaps," I told Inge, "we weren't meant to find her."

It was of little consolation to know that thousands of others shared my feelings of disappointment and discouragement. They had reached a similar dead-end in their searches. Like us, they wondered if they were meant to find their families. Perhaps it was best to leave things as they were. And yet, I wanted so much to know, at the very least, if my daughter was alive and whether or not she needed me.

11

A Search Begun and a Search Renewed

On Wednesday, Oct. 15, 1952, a Presbyterian minister and his wife entered the doors of Women's College Hospital in Toronto. They were both excited and apprehensive. For months, they had considered adopting a baby. Finally, having decided to do so, like any other expectant parents, they embarked upon the necessary preparations for the arrival of a young infant into their home. They prepared a room as a nursery with everything from crib to diapers. Soon they would see their adopted baby girl for the first time.

With their church background, it was logical that they had approached the Home for Unwed Mothers, established and maintained by the Presbyterian Church in Toronto. There, a young woman, far from her home in British Columbia, was awaiting the birth of her baby. She had already agreed to her child's adoption. Shortly after she gave birth to a healthy baby girl, the minister and his wife were told about the church background of both the mother and father. This information, plus a very brief medical history, convinced them to accept the baby.

At the hospital, they gratefully received their tiny new daughter. They returned with her to their home in Palmerston, a quiet town in the northwest corner of Wellington County, Ontario. The change this tiny child would bring to their lives was only half the story, for the mother was soon to learn that she was pregnant. She would give birth to a daughter of her own who would grow up as a sister to the young baby girl, now safe in a loving home. Carol had named her baby girl Catherine Anne. Her new parents renamed their adopted daughter Janet Elizabeth.

The lunch bell rang, signalling the end of morning classes. I eagerly walked the three blocks from school to my home for lunch. After eating, I turned on the television to watch "Father Knows Best" before I had to return to school. In that day's episode, Kathy, the youngest child in the "Father Knows Best" family, wondered if she was adopted. I enjoyed the program but I don't particularly remember relating the story to myself. However, after dinner that evening, I had an argument with Mom about something I forget now. In my usual fashion, I fled in tears and anger to my room.

I must have remembered the story I had seen on TV earlier that day for when I finally came downstairs I said to Mom, "You'll probably get mad at me again, but am I adopted?" I guess my mother felt the time had come for her to tell me the truth because she replied, "Yes, sit down and I'll tell you about it." I sat up on the kitchen counter and listened as by mother told me about the circumstances that had led to my adoption. Mom showed me a letter my birth mother had written when I was born, which she had left with the hospital. It contained information on both my biological mother and father. However, it provided little identifying information and was unsigned. I focused on the fact that my natural mother had studied music at university. She was unmarried. Mom told me that my biological father knew nothing about me. Both my natural parents were from out west.

What was most important was that Mom told me my birth mother's maiden name. I now realize how valuable this information was. Most adopted children, as well as their adoptive parents, never know the mother's name. I always remembered that name and repeated it over and over in my mind. I remembered the letter as well but not much of what it said. I mostly wanted to hear how Mom and Dad got me and where I was born.

Mom and I would imagine situations (more likely I made up the story and Mom would go along with it) about my conception. We would laugh and make light of it. Somewhere in time, as I was growing up, fantasy and reality became a little garbled.

From that time on, it was always my mother who answered my questions. My Dad ignored any discussion of adoption, seeming completely absorbed by the demands of his church. He was a wonderful minister and responded to the needs of his congregation, no matter what hour of the day or night. He was sensitive and caring and would do anything for anyone who needed help. Because of him, I became involved in the church and concerned with the well-being of others.

My Mom is as strong as any person can be and she would let me pester her with questions. My curiosity was insatiable and must have tested even her. She let me question her about the details of my adoption and early infancy. I never seemed to tire of hearing the story over and over again. She made me feel special. I grew up knowing that my background, whatever it might be, was not something about which I should feel ashamed.

I was amazed to discover that the parents of my friends already knew of my adoption. My family moved to Sarnia when I was three years old. They spoke to all the neighbours so they would not question my sister and me about our closeness in age. They also asked them not to tell me the truth about my origin.

After I did learn the truth about my adoption, and despite the love and security of my family, I always felt that I was somehow different. Neither my school friends nor Mom and Dad treated me any differently but the feeling was there. It was as if I belonged to my family, yet that I did not. My curiosity was never satisfied and the questions about my past returned again and again. These early thoughts and emotions never really left me. Through my adolescence and into adulthood, the idea that I really didn't know myself or who I was never subsided. To my family and friends I was a completely normal child and accepted as such but all along I continued musing about my origins.

My parents had lost their first two babies at birth. My sister was their third and she was special. She was conceived just prior to my birth and my Mom's pregnancy was difficult. The doctors were determined to deliver a healthy child to my parents and this, their third, was truly a blessing. As a result, I have always had a sister, seven months younger than I am. What is even more remarkable is that, as children, there was a physical likeness between us. My hair was slightly darker and I was taller and thinner but our facial features were as similar as any two biological sisters.

As small children, we were good friends. My sister was quiet and kept to herself more than I did. I tested anyone present with my nonstop chatter and tended to be a tattletale. She had a stubborn streak and wanted things to go her own way and this caused the typical sorts of sibling conflicts. My grandfather lived with us until he died and so my sister and I shared a bedroom for most of our school years.

From May to October every year, we were the same age and because we were so close in age we had many of the same friends. We were active in many of the same school and church functions. In spite of our closeness in age and our being raised like twins, our parents insisted that we be in separate classes in school. That was a decision that we both were grateful for since, after she accelerated in school, my sister was in the same grade as I was. In our early school years we dressed alike. We were frequently asked if we were twins and we would just smile. We were open about my adoption with our friends, but with people who did not know us well we would laugh and treasure our private secret.

We always received gifts together and often got the same things, although the colours would vary. When we were small, I always received gifts on my sister's birthday and vice versa. I remember the day I was visiting friends of my parents and their dog bit me in the face. For years following this accident my sister and I received gifts from them for every conceivable occasion.

It was not until late elementary school that our different interests became more pronounced. We shared clothes but seldom dressed alike any more and we wore our hair differently. However, we continued to be friends with neighbourhood girls and would often do things together. In high school we took different *subjects and our extracurricular activities were different. We knew many of the same people but also had different friends. When people question us now we often joke that we even shared boyfriends. In fact, that really wasn't true.*

As I grew up, my thoughts and questions about being adopted gradually faded, only to be reawakened every time I visited my grandparents in Toronto. Mom had told me I was born in Toronto and so visits there always made me look for someone who looked like me. Questions such as, who is my birth mother? or, do I have sisters or brothers? and a multitude of others jumped into my mind on each and every visit. My grandmother seemed to understand and helped me deal with these questions. She would take me in her arms and tell me that everyone loved me and I was special, just like my sister.

Teenage years can be a stormy time within any family and my experience was probably typical. The important difference for me was that I could find an easy excuse for my disagreements with my parents and sister. After all, I was different. I was adopted. I am sure that, in all families, siblings express their divergent interests, personalities and career plans during their teens. My sister's personality was closer to that of our parents. She was quiet and reserved. It was a challenge to penetrate her innermost thoughts and get her to open up. On the other hand, I shared everything and expressed all my feelings. As an adolescent, I was very insecure. I was desperate for affection and acceptance.

Slowly, my interests diverged from those of my family. I wanted to be a nurse. I pursued subjects in school which were not of great interest to either my sister or my parents. I never lost the feeling that I was different; in fact, I had a nagging notion that something was wrong with me. I felt the first urgings to search for my biological parents. But since I was busy and involved with other things, the desire to search diminished to the point where I seldom thought about it at all. University, nursing and, eventually, teacher's training occupied all my time.

I had known Ken for many years in school but it was while we were studying at the University of Western Ontario in London that we grew to love each other. Besides growing up in the same town, we had much in common. Ken was studying music and wanted to make it his career. I also loved music and had studied piano since I was a little girl. We decided to marry, even before we had completed university. We both knew that marriage would not keep us from completing our educations.

My father married us in his church, in Sarnia. We lived in married student residence, an apartment complex with one-bedroom apartments, and became totally occupied in finishing our studies and adjusting to married life together. I completely forgot about my earlier desire to search for my biological parents — until my son was born.

When you give birth to a baby, I think it is only natural to wonder what genes your child has inherited. New parents come face to face with this every day. It is particularly true when people look at your baby and try to determine who he looks like. I knew I would have to find my biological parents if I was ever to answer these questions. It was very important that I begin my search but I had just embarked upon the double responsibility of becoming a working mother. My determination to search was delayed again. I used to talk about it with my neighbour and she kept encouraging me to begin. In many ways, it was she who kept the idea alive.

My interest in searching became more active after Andrew's birth, particularly when I took him to his first eye doctor appointment. It was one thing to write "unknown" across my medical history but it was another to write it across my child's. During my pregnancy I had wondered what my child would inherit. It was a concern not to know what genetic imprints the child might receive. My motivation for searching never really changed. I wanted medical history but I also wondered what my birth parents were like.

I guessed that my parents must have been slim since I remained thin in spite of my eating or exercise patterns. I wondered about diseases like multiple sclerosis which would not have shown up until after my birth. I wondered why I was so sensitive and whether my parents were like that too.

Summer seems to have been a catalyst. One July, I contacted an organization that helps adopted children search for their birth parents. This involved regular meetings and a membership fee but did not seem to be what I was looking for. I had some information already, and I wasn't quite ready to share my story with a group of strangers. Often when in Toronto, I thought about my birth mother and wondered what secrets the university might hold about her. Ken and I had talked about making a trip for the sole purpose of finding out anything we could. But it was not until the summer of 1984 that we drove to Toronto with the single purpose of searching for information that might lead to my birth mother.

We had no luck at the music college which we believed my birth mother had attended. With a still enthusiastic spirit, we headed for the Almuni Office at the University of Toronto. I still remembered the maiden name of my birth mother from that day when my Mom first told me I was adopted. We met extremely friendly and helpful people and I told them that we were looking for the address of a former acquaintance of my aunt. I said she had graduated from the Faculty of Music sometime between 1953 and 1955.

A lady searched the computer files right then and there but found nobody by the name I remembered in those years. This not proving successful, she sent us to the library archives where they store the old yearbooks. We leafed through these books for a couple of hours. The possibility of seeing a picture of my mother was extremely exciting to me. Ken and I laughed together when we found the graduation pictures of both my adoptive parents, my aunt and several music professors whose classes Ken had attended at university.

We looked at hundreds of pictures from the years between 1948 and 1958 but none of them helped. Ken remembers now that one of the yearbooks was missing. It must have been 1952, a year we thought was too early. I began to question whether the information I had received about my mother was correct. I had never asked Mom about my birth mother's name since that first discussion so many years before. Now I thought that I could have mixed up the name. My aunt had also told me that she might have known my birth mother at university and that she thought Carol was her first name, but she was not absolutely certain. I was not even sure if my birth mother had, in fact, graduated. If she had, was it from the University of Toronto or the Royal Conservatory of Music, also located on the campus but not actually part of the university?

Ken and I enjoyed our day together but we were discouraged at not being any further ahead in our search. I knew my information was incorrect somewhere but I did not know where. Our summer holidays came to an end and we were busy with preparations for the next school year. Our search came to a temporary standstill.

Shortly after our third child, Rebecca, was born she became quite ill with bronchitis. Our son had also had difficulty with repeated bouts of bronchitis and asthma. There were signs that Becky was going to have similar bronchial problems. This led several family members and friends to make comments about the genes in my background, especially since Ken had no trace of allergies or respiratory ailments in his family, except a brother who suffered from seasonal hayfever.

One day Mom and I were discussing Becky's health. I asked her if I could have the letter my birth mother had left with the hospital when I was born. This was the first time I had mentioned the letter since I was a child. Much to my surprise, Mom immediately agreed and also said that I could have my adoption papers and my original birth certificate. I was stunned. I had not known before about my original birth certificate. It was a strange feeling when I looked at it and discovered that my birth mother had named me Catherine Anne.

I took the letter home with me and read it over and over again. It was handwritten and outlined some of the family background of my birth mother and father. It talked about a brother and sisters who would be my uncle and aunts. Most important, I now learned the exact year my birth mother graduated from university. It was earlier than I had thought. She had entered the University of Toronto in her second year and I was born at the *start of her final year. Other than that, the letter revealed nothing particularly new but it did clarify a few things. I treasured that letter. It was the only thing I had that was from my birth family.*

About this time, Ken completed arrangements to take a leave from his teaching duties, to complete his Master's degree. We would be spending the next year in Princeton, New Jersey. Putting our search plans aside again, we were suddenly busy packing everything that Ken, I and the three children would need for the next twelve months. We had to make arrangements to rent our house as well as the hundreds of things connected with such a move.

Late in July, just before we left, I had a feeling that if I did not try searching again now I never would. Not knowing where else to go, I once more telephoned the University of Toronto Alumni Office and asked if they would conduct another search for me. This time I could provide them with my birth mother's full name and her year of graduation. I spoke to the same lady who had been so helpful at the time of our earlier inquiries. She told me to call her back in a few days to give her time to look through the records.

When I called again, she told me there was a woman of that name who had graduated in 1953 from the Faculty of Music. She said that she had kept in touch with the alumni association and now lived out west. My heart leaped and I started shaking with excitement. One of the things mentioned in my birth mother's letter was that she and her brother had attended an art school out west in the summers. I was sure that this woman was the one I was searching for. The Alumni Office would not give me her address but said that they would forward a letter for me. It was Ken's turn to take over.

We had discussed several times what we would do if the opportunity ever arose to make contact. Ken had always wanted to be the contact person and to approach the subject through our common love of music. But now I was apprehensive. I did not know whether I should go through with this.

One of my biggest concerns and reasons for hesitating in making contact was my fear of causing friction in a marriage should my mother's husband and family not know of my birth.

However, the Alumni Office had informed me that the woman I was trying to locate was divorced. Perhaps my approach to her would therefore not be as disruptive as I feared.

Ken wrote a letter explaining that he was a music teacher, that he was married with three children, and that his wife was adopted. He said that searching and contacting her was his idea and that I supported his wish to find her. He also stated that I did not know that he was writing to her. He said that if she was the woman he was seeking and, if she wished to correspond, she could contact him at his school. He very tactfully left her with all the options. This letter was not completely truthful in that I was fully aware of its contents. But we both felt that she would find it easier to contact Ken, either with a positive or negative reaction, if she thought that I was unaware of his approach.

Ken drove all the way to Toronto to take the letter to the Alumni Office where they would forward it. A few days later, we left for Princeton. Although I tried not to think of what might or might not happen as a result of the letter, not a day passed when I did not wonder about what the reaction was going to be. Of course, I also wanted to know whether this woman was, in fact, my mother.

12

What Do You Do When You Meet Your Daughter?

The spring of 1985 brought with it not just a renewal of nature's promise but also a new determination to continue my search. The painful disappointment of the past winter had lifted. I had collected a lot of material that could still prove useful and, although I had failed to identify my daughter, I remained convinced that I was on the right track. There were a lot of avenues still open and there were several areas where I felt that either my own research or the detective's was faulty or incomplete.

I brought out all the files and tried to figure out where I might have gone wrong. I reviewed all my own efforts as well as those of the detective. Finally, I concluded that there were a number of specific things that should be done to refine the material I had already assembled. Only then should I venture into other possible areas of research. Much of the new material I required could be gathered only in Ontario. I was not now free to go there myself. As I was not happy with the work done by the first detective, I contacted a different agency.

I asked the new detective to double check all the baptismal and Sunday School records of the Protestant churches in the county, particularly all the Presbyterian churches. It seemed to me a church-going family would have their adopted child baptized and christened. And I was certain that an agency like the Presbyterian Home for Unwed

Mothers would allow a child to be adopted only into a church home. I told the detective to examine the records over a two-year period, beginning with the date of Catherine Anne's birth.

In addition, I asked him to collect the names of all church ministers and other paid church employees living in the county at the time of the adoption. The church connection had grown strong in my mind because I felt that it was something I had not given enough attention to at the start of my own investigation. While he was undertaking this assignment, I would begin work on creating a list of all schoolteachers who were working in the area at the time. I would add them to my list of professionals.

The other thing I wanted to do was pursue my earlier plan and place advertisements in the Ontario newspapers on the date of Catherine Anne's birthday. In a few months, she would be thirty-three. I still had time to prepare an attention-grabbing advertisement and arrange for its placement in the fall.

Before receiving any new reports from the detective, Inge and I embarked upon a ten-day tour of British Columbia with visiting friends from Holland. We drove through the Fraser Canyon and into the Caribou, across to Jasper and down the scenic highway to Banff. Any response from the detective was far from my mind as we went on to enjoy the Sushwap and Okanagan, arriving back home refreshed by the magnificent scenery we had shared with our friends.

Entering the house, we unpacked, patted the cats and checked the mail. It was mostly the usual collection of leaflets and flyers along with the unwelcome bills. I could see no reply from the detective but it was possibly too early for that. Two or three personal letters took priority. One in particular caught my immediate attention. It was from Carol.

Our friends were busy bringing the suitcases into the house and removing the accumulated debris from the van we had rented for our trip. I took Carol's letter with me onto the sundeck so I could read it in some privacy. What her letter contained was the most exciting news I had heard since our meeting four years before, when she had first told me about Catherine Anne.

It was a short note. She wrote that she had received a letter from a man inquiring about whether she could possibly be the mother of a woman, now thirty-two years of age, who had been given up for adoption in 1952. The letter went on to state that he had been searching for his wife's natural mother for some time. His investigations had led him to Carol.

I yelled for Inge to join me on the sundeck, startling our visitors in the process since they had no idea what all the excitement was about. I quickly showed her the letter which she read in a minute. When she had finished, she rushed towards me, throwing her arms around my neck, shouting, "We've found her — we've found her!"

"Not really," I said, "it looks like she's found us."

"I don't care — I don't care," she continued, "we've found her. That's all that matters."

Inge's eyes were full of tears but I have never seen her happier. We hugged and laughed and cried as we began voicing a host of questions, interrupting each other in a jumble of words.

By this time our guests were totally alarmed by our performance. They were completely ignorant of Catherine Anne's existence, let alone our search for her or the significance of the news we had just received. I left Inge to provide an explanation for our unusual behavior while I phoned Carol.

She had been trying to contact me but, of course, we had been away on our trip. I crossed my fingers that she would be home. I was so excited that I don't know what I would have done if there had been no answer to my call.

Fortunately, Carol was home. She sounded every bit as excited as I felt. While she had not taken an active part in my four-year search she had carried the secret of Catherine Anne far longer than I had. The letter she had received was much more than she had ever expected when she first told me about our daughter. She now knew that she was not only alive and well but wanted to communicate with her. I could hear the relief and happiness in her voice.

Since she did not know where I was or how long it would take me to respond to her letter, Carol had already replied telling the writer that she was, in all probability, the woman he was seeking. She also stated that she would welcome any contact or communication with her daughter.

The letter Carol had received also provided a lot of information about the woman we both now felt must certainly be Catherine Anne. Her husband was a music teacher and choral director in Ontario. They were currently living in Princeton, New Jersey, where he was studying for his Master's degree in music. The next bit of information was a little startling. They had three children, a boy and two girls — making me an instant grandfather. The wives of two of my sons were expecting at the time so I was beginning to prepare myself for the grandfather role. This bit of news, however, was a little overwhelming.

After so many years and so many expectations dashed by disappointment the search appeared to be over. The news was far better than we had ever hoped for. Our daughter was alive and well, happily married with three young children. It even appeared that she had developed a love of and interest in music, with a husband who had pursued a musical career. It was hard to imagine a happier ending to our search. As Carol had already replied to the letter, there was little I could do now but wait to see what developed.

By this time, Inge had given a brief explanation to our guests of what was going on. Along with Inge, they were now waiting for me to repeat everything Carol had told me. It was wonderfully exciting and Inge and I could hardly contain our emotions. We had spent so many hours and so much effort on the search. Now all the time, money and disappointment had suddenly become insignificant. Our search had failed but that didn't matter because Catherine Anne had found us. We now had to wait patiently for direct contact from her.

One day, during the first week of our stay in Princeton, Ken collected the mail and took one of the letters upstairs. A few minutes later, he came down again and said, "This is what you've been waiting for." My heart pounded as I read and reread the letter. The woman we had located through the Alumni Office was, in fact, the person I had been searching for over so many years.

The only question she asked was my birth date. Ken had neglected to include it in the letter. I found out that not only was she my mother but that she wanted to get to know me, if that was what I wanted. Nothing was more important than answering her letter so I dropped everything and sat down to compose a response.

My first letter to Carol was an extremely condensed account of my life and family. Ken wrote as well. He wanted to explain why he had acted as intermediary, leading her to believe that I was unaware of the letter. Once more, I found myself waiting impatiently for a reply. I wanted desperately to get to know and become friends with my mother. However, I didn't want to force myself upon her in any way. As it happened, Carol was as anxious as I was to catch up on all the lost years. We discovered that we wanted to share all that had happened in the thirty-three years since my birth.

Carol received a reply to her letter within a few days and the waiting was over. There was now no doubt. This time, our daughter signed the letter herself. The first thing we had to get used to was her name, not Catherine or Catherine Anne but Janet, the name given to her by her adoptive parents. Her letter was kind and thoughtful.

Our subsequent letters were filled with emotion, awe and a growing respect and love for each other. I shed many tears as I read of what Carol had endured to give me life. I grew to appreciate more each day her character, strength, and love, and quickly became familiar with her life and family. I also grew to appreciate more the love of the family I had grown up with.

I took the time to examine my childhood more closely and tried to understand more fully the risk and commitment undertaken by adoptive parents. As our stories came together I realized that not only was I fortunate to have grown up in a loving family but I now had a biological mother who, along with her son and two daughters, also welcomed me into their family.

Early in our correspondence, Carol told me about my father. He had been unaware of my existence until just a few years before when, being in Calgary on business, he had taken her out to dinner. Only then did she reveal to him that, when they had parted thirty years before, she had been pregnant and, later, had given me up for adoption.

Carol told me that my father's name was Barrie and that he lived in Vancouver. She mentioned that she had already talked on the phone with him about Ken's letter. Therefore, he already knew that I had found Carol and that I wanted also to make contact with him. Now I had to sit down and compose another letter of introduction — this time, to my biological father.

Janet had told Carol that she would immediately write to me as well. I was going to have to be patient but I knew her birthday was coming up in just a few days. From the day Carol told me about our daughter, October 7th had become a special day for me, invoking very conflicting feelings. This year again, my daughter would be on my mind throughout the day. Once more I would wonder about how she was, where she lived, what she looked like and all the other questions that had been with me since I had first learned of her existence.

I now had the answers to many of these questions and her birthday had become even more important to me.

What do fathers do for their daughters on their birthday? This was not a normal situation. I had never met or spoken to my daughter. Finally, I arranged for a dozen roses to be delivered to her in Princeton, along with a short note.

That two- or three-line note took me an hour to compose. I still had not heard directly from Janet and I wasn't even sure that she wanted to have anything to do with me. I settled for a rather standard birthday wish and an invitation to communicate with me if that was her desire.

A few days later, her first letter to me arrived. It was full of news about her early life, her years at school and university, how she had met her husband and, of course, about her three children. She enclosed a picture of herself holding her youngest girl. Inge and I stared and stared at that picture, the first visual evidence I had seen of my daughter.

This was a picture of the daughter we had been searching for all these years. I was astonished at my reaction. I was overwhelmed by a feeling of parental love for this woman I had yet to meet personally. It was as if she had been a part of my family from the beginning. Inge and I discussed how that picture evoked a desire to protect and, most of all, the unconditional love that parenthood inspires.

I wanted to hear her voice and so, after rereading her letter, I telephoned Princeton. Ken answered the call which I had placed person-to-person to Janet. I heard him call for her and say, "It's from Vancouver for you." When she came on the line, for one of the first times in my life I was almost speechless. I can't remember now what our first words were to each other but we both gradually settled down and we had a long conversation. We were both full of questions about our respective searches. I also wanted to know more about her childhood, her school years and countless small but important details of her life.

As it happened, my birthday arrived a few days after I posted the letter to my father. Answering a knock at the door that morning,

I was presented with a box containing one dozen long-stemmed roses and a short note from Barrie, wishing me a happy birthday. I had made friends with my neighbour and I brought her over to see the flowers. We were in shock at the whole thing. I was surprised that a father I never knew would care about me.

A couple of days later, Barrie phoned from Vancouver. He had received my letter and wanted to assure me that he welcomed me as a daughter. He hoped we would soon meet and get to know each other. I was shaking and could hardly talk on the phone. I was already trying to cope with hearing from Carol and the way Barrie responded was the one thing I really hadn't prepared myself for. After the call, I was a blithering idiot. I was elated, bewildered and confused as to what would happen next. I was not at all sure what contacting Carol was going to lead to.

Over the next weeks, letters from both Carol and Barrie provided me with overwhelming information and details about my new-found relatives and the history and background of the two sides of my biological family. I tried to piece together all this new knowledge. I could hardly absorb all the information I was receiving. For years, I had had only dreams. Now, in a matter of months, I knew more about myself and my past than I could readily grasp.

I stared long and hard at the first pictures I received of Carol and Barrie. One was of the two of them at a formal dance and I stared and stared at it. I was totally amazed and humbled that not only had Barrie accepted his new knowledge that he had a daughter but that he had spent considerable time and money searching for me. It was hard to believe that I was the object of that search.

Carol and I had come to know each other about as well as one can through correspondence. In fact, a certain comfort zone had grown in small ways. At the beginning, our words were carefully chosen and we rewrote our letters several times to avoid mistakes. But as time went on we were more able to write freely about our thoughts. I was also developing a closeness with Barrie and his wife Inge. However, we were surprised and delighted, but also apprehensive, when they proposed flying to Princeton just before Christmas to meet us.

Now we had to tell our children about their new grandparents. I had always freely discussed my adoption with Andrew and he was full of questions as he eagerly looked forward to meeting yet another grandma and grandpa. Kim, only four at the time, just took the news as an ordinary everyday occurrence. Becky was still a baby and too young to understand.

We exchanged a couple more letters but Inge and I desperately longed to meet Janet, her husband and children. Letters and phone calls were no longer enough, and we decided to fly to Princeton just before Christmas. We counted the days before we would actually meet this young woman who had occupied so much of our thoughts for such a long time. Finally, we boarded the flight to Chicago, where we transferred to a smaller plane that would land at the local airport not far from their home.

As we neared our destination, knowing Janet would be meeting us at the airport, I suddenly became very nervous. I asked Inge, "What do you do when you meet your daughter?" It probably sounds silly now but I was really wondering what to do. "Do I shake hands?"

"Don't worry about it," she replied, "you'll know what to do when you see her."

We were taxiing toward the small terminal building. In just a few minutes, I would meet my daughter. As the plane came to a stop, I could see through the window into the waiting room. I recognized Janet from the picture she had sent me. She was waiting by the door with her small baby in her arms. Inge and I collected our hand luggage and headed for the stairs.

My neighbour in Princeton was extremely supportive and excited as the day grew near when I would meet my father for the first time. She babysat Andrew and Kim while Ken and I took Becky with us to the airport. Princeton Airport is very small and

I knew that I would have no difficulty recognizing Barrie and Inge, from the pictures they had sent us earlier. My stomach was turning somersaults as the plane landed. I was not sure if there was any proper etiquette for such an event and so I had to let instinct take over. I hoped that I would not make some inappropriate gesture on our first hello.

Ken hung in the background and I held Becky.

Inge came through the door first, then Barrie.

We all greeted each other with a hug, and a feeling of camaraderie was instantly established.

Inge went first and we had no sooner entered the waiting room when Janet and the baby were in my arms. I was holding my daughter for the first time.

We spent three glorious days together. There were no difficulties or awkward moments. I liked Janet's husband immediately and their three children — my grandchildren — were an absolute delight. Janet and I spent hours together, filling in the gaps. I gave her a brief description of the dozens of relatives she had suddenly acquired. She told me of the wonderful couple who had adopted and cared for her.

The hardest thing was to look at each other. I wanted to study Barrie's face but not stare. I couldn't help wonder if Barrie was disappointed now that we had seen each other in person. I knew I wasn't. We shared many wonderful stories over walks and dinners. The children established a mutual friendship and growing admiration for their new grandparents as they strung Christmas lights and read stories together.

Janet explained how her search had led to success and we tried to figure out why my search had failed. The reason was just what I had feared when I first prepared my lists of girls and professionals. Janet's family had moved from Wellington County when she was barely three years old. She had never attended school there. Her father had accepted a call to a church in Sarnia, which was not too far away but was outside the area of my investigations. It was there that Janet had gone to school. I later checked my files and lists and, sure enough, there was the name of Janet's adoptive father.

My mind went back to a day almost fours years earlier when I had experienced such a warm feeling about the town of Palmerston. I had been walking down the main street looking for a coffee shop. This was where Janet's adopting parents lived when they brought her home from the hospital. I had been correct in concluding that they had lived in one of those towns I had visited. Janet and I both wondered whether I would have found her in my renewed search. I remembered that I had instructed the detective to investigate all Presbyterian ministers and check all the church baptismal records.

It didn't matter. We were together now. We went for a long walk near the beautiful campus of Princeton University. For December, it was a warm sunny afternoon and I felt wonderful. We didn't have the slightest difficulty talking to each other. Inge and Ken made Janet and me sit beside each other and laughed at the obvious family resemblance. "Well, if you had any idea of denying she's your daughter, forget it," Inge joked.

The children were full of questions, particularly Andrew, Janet's seven-year-old son and my oldest grandchild. On the second day, he had invited a young friend over to play. The adult conversation in the room ceased abruptly when we heard his friend ask, "Who are these people?" Without a moment's hesitation Andrew responded, "Oh, my Mom's adopted and that's her real father." A straight-forward answer to a direct question. We did not need to say anything more. The two boys just accepted what was fact and went on with their play. The rest of us laughed together at how easily young children deal with situations that can tie up adults in the tightest of knots.

We did realize, however, that there was going to be some difficulty for the children with so many grandparents. How would they refer to us all without total confusion? Inge eventually provided the solution when she introduced the children to the Dutch names for Grandma and Grandpa. Oma and Opa we would be and have been ever since.

13

Instant Family

The time flew by and what we had looked forward to for the past months was over very quickly. As Barrie and Inge left, we made plans to come west the next summer, to meet Carol and her family in Calgary and then continue on to Vancouver. Once again, more thoughts and dreams were in the making.

During the wonderfully fulfilling time of getting acquainted with Carol and Barrie, one thought lingered in the background that caused me many nights of sleeplessness. I wondered what we had begun and how it would affect my adoptive parents. Up to this time, they had no idea what was going on.

My parents had led me to believe that searching for my biological parents was not an acceptable thing to do. Although we had never openly talked about it, I felt that if they discovered I was searching it would hurt them terribly. When I decided to go ahead it was with the clear understanding that I was not looking for parent substitution. I was looking for medical information and for answers to questions I had carried with me since I was a child. I now could only hope that Mom and Dad knew I loved them and that what had occurred would in no way change the way I felt about them.

Now that I had found my birth parents, I did not want to do anything to make my adoptive parents feel rejected. In fact, I now felt much closer to them than ever and I wanted them to know that. Finally, after much discussion and many letters that were never mailed, Ken and I agreed that we owed Mom and Dad the *courtesy of telling them in person. We decided to keep our news to ourselves until we returned home in June.*

The day we told my parents will always remain with me. They were wonderful. Dad was quiet. Mom asked a few questions. It could have been a strained, tense and horribly awkward situation but Mom kept the atmosphere as comfortable as possible. My parents have always thought things over very carefully before making any judgments. On this occasion, they kept most of their thoughts to themselves. As for me, it was a great relief knowing that there were no more secrets. I could now talk openly about Carol and Barrie, although I purposely refrained from doing so too often. Mom and Dad asked for Carol and Barrie's addresses so they might write to both of them. They did this a few days later.

July came and it was time for us to fly west to meet Carol and her family. Sometimes the restlessness of children is a blessing, and the flight was one of those times. I was kept too busy to worry about how the meeting with my mother would go. However, as soon as the plane began its descent, I was again consumed with excitement. Suddenly we had landed and Carol, along with my new brother and sister, were there to greet us. Ken saw them first. We had exchanged pictures, but seeing them in real life was totally different. In my excitement, I didn't recognize my sister from her picture. My brother had such a gentle and warm face that I instantly felt comfortable with him. Seeing Carol fulfilled every dream.

During the next few days, we shared pictures and stories of our past. Carol wanted me to get a feeling for my ancestry and she couldn't have found a more willing or appreciative audience. I already felt a real closeness with my new family. I immediately liked my new brother and sister, and my children were thrilled with their new cousins, aunts, uncle and grandma.

I had sensed a real inner strength and tenderness about Carol in her letters. Now I was seeing these qualities as I never had before. I felt so proud to know where I had come from.

We were sad to leave but now knew that we would all see each other many times again. We travelled on to Vancouver where we stayed with Barrie and Inge. There I met three more brothers and their wives.

The months immediately following our trip to Princeton were exciting for both of us. The wives of two of our sons presented us with beautiful granddaughters. Our family was expanding so rapidly we could hardly keep pace. With Janet and Ken and their family arriving in July we were to be host for the first time to three very lively, energetic and active grandchildren. The first thing we did was make the house child-proof. I barricaded the stair-wells and filled in the gaps in the sundeck railings so tiny children could not accidentally slip through to the creek below.

We borrowed a crib from friends and I spent a hilarious hour trying to put it together. It is amazing how one soon forgets such basic child-rearing skills. The two older children would sleep in sleeping bags on mattresses in the recreation room. I soon learned how popular that was when they discovered their own TV set and an old-fashioned pinball machine. In the meantime Inge baked enough chocolate chip cookies to feed an army.

It was great fun having the family with us. The house rang with the sounds of happy children and I began to learn my grandfathering skills. I sawed up some pieces of wood and showed Andrew and Kim how to make little ferry boats. Down at the pond in the backyard we sailed make-believe cars and passengers from one end to the other. I had bought some small cedar tables for use on the sundeck but they needed staining. I set the children on a large plastic sheet in the garage, gave them each a paint brush, and set them loose. Afterwards, Inge and Janet had to stand them in the sink and wash off the stain since they looked like little Indians on the warpath.

One weekend, Janet was inundated with a host of aunts, uncles, cousins and her only surviving grandmother. I had warned her that all the relatives were very curious and that she would be under inspection. I must confess I sat back and watched with fascination. The young babies and children were the center of attention, instantly bridging any awkwardness between the young mothers. Janet's youngest daughter was barely walking and she was into everything. She was fascinated by our two cats and insisted on following one or the other wherever they went. For the children, it was just like any other family gathering.

My sisters and their husbands were used to my public adventures and I'm sure that nothing would have surprised them by now.

They simply sat back and enjoyed the occasion. What was most interesting was the reaction of my sons to their sister. Janet was a wise older sister and let them take their time. Then, almost before we knew it, there were shouts of laughter as they began comparing everything from eyes and ears to hair colour.

I had always had a small brown spot in my right eye and they discovered that Janet had one as well. However, it was the Clark thumb that received the most attention. Like my father, I had a very short thumb which I had duly passed on to my sons. Janet's wasn't quite as short but her oldest son showed the same strength of genes. His new uncles made him show off the family trait. He obviously enjoyed being the center of attention.

Of course, it wasn't as if Janet and her brothers had grown up together. It would take some time before any feelings of closeness would develop, but there was no doubt about the blood tie. They had seen each other for themselves and needed no further proof. Suddenly, I was the butt of their jokes. "Hey Dad, have you got any more surprises up your sleeve for us?" one of them shouted. I assured them all that I did not.

Meeting all my new relatives was terrific and not too terrifying. The hardest part was trying not to stumble over my words in my attempt to seem normal. I was so grateful for the two babies who took most of the attention away from me. I felt very comfortable with everyone. My wishes were and still remain that I could get to know my brothers on more than a superficial level. I never had brothers and I would love to be close enough to them to share ideas, experiences and feelings. I would also love to get to know my sisters-in-law better and have the cousins know each other.

A few days after her arrival, Janet telephoned a university friend who now lived in Vancouver. I was standing near her as her friend asked her why she was staying at my home. I obviously couldn't hear the question but I saw Janet look across at me and say, "Because he's my father." I felt a surge of pride and was deeply grateful.

The time we had together flew past but, before Janet and her family had to return home, we all felt quite comfortable together. While I couldn't get over the awe of actually having Janet with me, we were beginning to be less cautious with each other. It already seemed quite normal and nothing unusual to have my daughter and her family visiting from out of town. A special bonus was getting to know Ken. Sharing a love of music, we had much to talk about. We discovered that, over the years, we had sung much of the same music — although he now far exceeded my skill and knowledge.

The children, in particular, seemed to adapt easily to a host of new relatives. They seemed quite happy with the fact that they had acquired yet more grandparents. On our part, we took note of birth dates for future presents and tried to remember their wishes for favorite toys and games. We learned that becoming instant grandparents required a lot of catching up about the latest children's TV programs and all the weird and wonderful characters they employed. We settled down to the routine faced by all families whose children become separated by distance. Letters and telephone calls had to make up for personal visits.

We still had not met Janet's adoptive parents and this was something both Inge and I had wanted to do for some time. I had already written them in an attempt to express my deep appreciation for the care and support they had provided for my daughter. This was a difficult letter to compose. My feelings toward them were heartfelt. Having raised my three sons, I knew the sacrifice and dedication required of parents. I wanted them to know how I felt, while at the same time assuring them that I had no wish to replace them in Janet's affections.

Several of my friends and acquaintances had adopted children. Since learning about my daughter, I had done a lot of thinking about the role of adopting parents. To many couples, the discovery of an inability to produce a child of their own is a tragic and shattering experience. Many a marriage has failed to survive such a test. Deciding to adopt someone else's child is a difficult decision, requiring a loving dedication and commitment. In addition, the resources and training needed are the same, as if the child was their very own.

Raising children certainly has its rewards but I often wonder how many parents would do it over again. It is an eighteen- to twenty-year obligation. You must see to their health and education, nurse their bruised knees and egos and watch patiently as they defiantly insist on experiencing for themselves all the errors and mistakes you have warned them to avoid. They become part of you. You share their feelings of joy and sorrow, success and heartbreak. Many adopting parents have told me they soon forget that their child, now occupying so much of their time and attention, is not actually their own flesh and blood.

It is easy to imagine the questions that arise when adoptive parents first learn of their child's desire to find his or her natural parents.

"Why would you want to find them? Aren't we your real mother and father?"

"What have we done to deserve this?"

"Haven't you been happy here after all we've done for you?"

"Don't you love us?"

"They gave you away, what can you possibly gain by contacting them?"

All too often, an adopted child is unable to articulate the real reasons for wanting to begin such a search until much later. And unfortunately, not all adopting parents anticipate this event and are shocked by it. On the other hand, I have also met adoptive parents who have encouraged their child's wishes and dreams. They have joined in the detective work that followed the decision to search with dedication and encouragement.

The fear most frequently expressed by adoptive parents is that blood parents will rob them of their child's affections. During my research for this book I met with hundreds of adoptees and their adoptive parents. I did not discover a single instance of children turning their backs on their adoptive parents once they found their natural parents. Nonetheless, the fear of this happening remains the foremost objection raised by adoptive parents' associations who oppose any change in our adoption laws that would result in open records, and thus, more reunions.

I wanted to discuss my thoughts with Gwen and George Young, the Presbyterian minister and his wife who had devoted so much of their lives to raising my daughter. If possible, I wanted to reassure them that, in no way, did I want to interfere in the close relationship that existed between them and Janet. I wanted them to feel a part of the nuclear family that was continuing to grow as a result of Janet having met Carol and me.

The opportunity to meet them for the first time finally presented itself when Ken, having completed all the work for his postgraduate degree, was about to stage a graduation concert. He invited us to attend. We spent a week in London, Ontario, where Ken and Janet had now made their home and established firm roots. It was reassuring to see their home and to realize how secure they were in their work and community life. We visited the school where Janet taught preschool, met their neighbours and enjoyed doing normal family things together. One night we brought in Chinese food for a family dinner. The next day, we spent a wonderful afternoon with the children at a maple sugar farm. It seemed so natural to be with them — by now we really were all part of the same family.

Ken's concert was held in a large church. His school and university choirs massed together to fill a third of the auditorium. We agreed that Janet would sit with her adoptive parents near the front while Inge and I adjourned to the balcony. We would join them at the reception to follow later in the adjoining hall, at which time Janet would introduce us. Janet was apprehensive about the meeting since she desperately wanted us all to like each other.

The concert was a spectacular success. The audience, made up of Ken's friends and the singers' parents, gave him a standing ovation for completing his degree, providing us all with a wonderful evening of music, and for contributing so much to the musical life of the community. An incident during intermission made me chuckle. Inge had left the church for some fresh air. I was left sitting beside a woman who was the mother of one of the girls in the choir. She asked me if I was also the parent of one of the participants. I hesitated, not knowing quite how to respond. "Not one of the choir members," I replied, "but I am related to one of the participants."

She looked at me closely and suddenly stated, "You're Janet's father, aren't you?"

I was dumbfounded. "Yes," I spluttered, "but how did you know that?"

"Just by looking at you," she answered.

It turned out that she had never met Janet's adoptive parents and knew nothing of our amazing story. Since there wasn't any secret about it, I decided to give her a brief explanation of how I came to be attending the concert. Like so many others, she found our story like a fairy tale. Also attending the concert and accompanying us that evening was Carol's youngest daughter, Janet's half-sister. She was living with Janet and Ken while completing her year at university. I introduced her to the woman beside me just as the concert got underway again. I had the feeling this woman could hardly wait for it to end so she could tell others about the unusual group she had sat beside that evening.

We followed everyone into the church hall to congratulate Ken, who was positively beaming at the success of the evening. Because a lineup of others wanted to speak to him we moved over to Janet, who then introduced us to the Reverend Mr. and Mrs. Young, her adoptive parents. The ice was broken by our mutual agreement that the evening's concert had been something very special. Very quickly, we were on a first name basis and Janet, looking visibly relieved, turned to her other guests. We agreed to meet with Gwen and George the next day when we would have a better opportunity to talk.

At that and later meetings we were able to piece together the story of how Janet came into their care. Like most other adopting parents, they believed that they were unable to have children of their own. They visited several adoption agencies in Toronto, one of them being the Presbyterian Home for Unwed Mothers where Carol was staying at the time. Of course, they did not meet Carol but they did learn a lot about both of us. Our church backgrounds played a role in their decision to adopt Janet. Soon after, Gwen learned she was pregnant but they easily adjusted to the responsibility of raising two daughters.

When the girls were young, they explained the closeness in their ages by telling their friends that they had adopted Janet. Later, wanting the girls to grow up as sisters, they avoided the subject within the family itself until the appropriate time came to reveal to Janet the truth about her background. Gwen remembers the day well when Janet, then ten years old, came into her kitchen and asked her directly if she was adopted. She sat up on the counter and Gwen told her about losing two pregnancies and how much she and George wanted a little girl. She told about how they had decided to adopt her after learning about her parents and their background. She described how they went to the hospital in Toronto to get her, and assured her that she was very special to them.

Gwen told us that, from that time on, Janet seldom raised the subject of adoption. When she did, they dealt with it in a very matter-of-fact way. Janet and her sister grew up as close friends in a happy and secure family. As she had already explained to me, Janet did not mention her search for Carol and me until after we had all been in communication. Gwen and George told me that they were quite surprised, but also very pleased for Janet's sake. She now had answers to all her questions. They shared her excitement at meeting all her new relatives. At no time did they feel threatened by the reunion. In fact, their relationship with Janet has been enhanced and they feel closer to her than ever.

I laughed when I learned that they had been every bit as apprehensive about meeting us as we were about meeting them. After the concert, they were quite nervous because they didn't want to do anything or make any mistakes that might hurt Janet. This was exactly how Inge and I had felt. Since that tense first meeting, our relationship has become quite natural with regular exchanges of letters and visits. Some months later, Carol also had the opportunity to meet Gwen and George. Our family circle continued to grow, all of us enriched by the experience.

Most important of all, there was the peace in knowing my daughter was alive, well and happy.

After so much has happened, I now realize that as I was growing up I always felt not only different, but deficient in some way. When I was studying guidance at teacher's college I met a young high school girl who was adopted and going through a real identity crisis. She felt that she belonged to nobody. I could empathize with her when she told me that she felt abandoned and odd. I have since come to realize this is a common experience among the adopted.

While adopted children do not have the knowledge about themselves that all other children take for granted, they are also the only children who can fantasize about a different set of parents and a different life. They also know that there is a chance, no matter how remote, of making their fantasy come true. However, teenage years can be extremely difficult for all children. I don't feel that this is the proper time for them to become embroiled in all the apprehensions and tensions of a reunion. I don't think that a teenager has the emotional stability to handle what he or she may find.

I still get nervous when I talk to Barrie and Carol. I'm still afraid that I will say or do the wrong thing. I'm thankful I took the risk and started searching. I thought I might discover the worst but, instead, life has been especially good to me. I have been blessed with a fairytale story. The time was right.

After all the searching, the excitement, the disappointments and the wonder of meeting Janet, an angry thought remained with me. It was as intense as when I first set out to find her. Ontario's adoption laws, like those of most other provinces, prevented an easy reunion of mature adults who wanted very much to meet. Everyone at government level said that none of us — father, mother or daughter — should be helped in achieving our goal. Every time I thought about their attitude, I would feel the resentment rising inside me.

I have been a part of government both as an elected representative and as a bureaucrat, and I know how impersonal government can be. There is no compassion or understanding in adoption law for circumstances like mine. There is no comprehension of what the secrecy and deceit is doing to human beings who simply want to discover their roots.

As a man in my mid-fifties, I had no right to enter an office and examine the records about my daughter. As a woman in her thirties, Janet had no right to examine her own file so that she could identify her natural mother. This information was in the files, held by public servants in trust. For whom? Government maintained it knew better than Janet or I just what was in our best interest and what we should know about each other. I cannot accept this. If for no other reason, I cannot accept it because of all those people I have met who are still searching.

14

A Plea for Reform

When I began the search for my daughter I had no idea of the size of the adopted family. It has been estimated that as many as one million adoptees are living in Canada today, and that one in five North Americans has a direct tie to adoption by family relationship or close friendship. I also had no conception of the number of sons and daughters, mothers and fathers who are actively searching for their blood relatives.

Adoption law as we know it in Canada is quite recent. From feudal times the English, maintaining that property passed through blood lines only, strongly rejected any legal recognition of adoption. They also held strong beliefs that one was born into a class. There was no other means of entry into it. Canadians inherited this tradition and opposed any formal adoption practice until after World War I, when they faced an alarming increase in the number of unwanted babies and young children. It was not the welfare of these children that first caught society's attention, but rather the prospect that the taxpayer would have to pay for the cost of building and maintaining orphanages or similar institutions for these children. Near desperation, governments in all the provinces looked for alternate means of support for unwanted children. A system of adoption seemed to be the perfect solution and by the early 1920s, most of the provinces had introduced adoption legislation.

Professional social workers felt that adoption could succeed only if the children concerned joined their new families under the cloak of absolute secrecy. What the children might think of this when they themselves became adults was not considered. The social workers said it was in the children's best interests never to learn of their sinful origin. As a result, most parents never told their children about their adoption.

The motivation behind this secrecy was not concern for the child but rather the fears of the adults involved in the process. The new father and mother wanted secrecy so the adoption of a child would not prompt questions about their fertility. Likewise, it was essential to protect the birth mother through secrecy so that she could go on to establish a proper marriage and family of her own. Consequently, society and the law proclaimed the impossible — that by adoption, a child would become the actual blood child of the adoptive parents. British Columbia led the way in 1957 by declaring that, upon adoption, a child "for all purposes" was the child of his adoptive parents and ceased to be the child of his natural parents.

Over the years, Canadians have abandoned many of these old notions but the rationale for them — the need for secrecy — has lived on. To this day, requests to open adoption records meet with firm opposition from both government and the courts.

In talking to people in the adoption reform movement, I have come across few demands for an end to adoption. Most of them consider it the best way to bring together unwanted or neglected children and caring parents who are willing to share their home and affection. What these people do demand, however, is an end to the secrecy and falsehoods that still surround every adoption. I can only agree that the time has come to change the concept and practice of adoption to something that is open and honest and in the best interest of the child involved.

Most natural children have always known who their mother and father are. If they have brothers or sisters, they have grown up with them. In most cases they have known their grandparents and numerous aunts, uncles and cousins. They have also learned where their ancestors were born and from where they emigrated. Upon reaching maturity, most natural children have absorbed, albeit unconsciously, countless pieces of family information over the years. From this knowledge, they have created an identity which enables them to know who they are and how they fit into society at large. Some people argue that adopted children have this same knowledge and security within the structure of their adopted families — but it has become clear in recent years that, for many adoptees, this simply is not the case.

The natural inborn desire to know where one fits into the scheme of things often prompts adopted children to demand the same rights as the natural child. They do not wish to turn their backs on their adopted families — in many cases, they are as curious about the family backgrounds of their adopted family as they are of their natural family.

The most outspoken opposition to any change in adoption law comes from two sources: adoptive parents and, more recently, the Pro Life movement. As for adoptive parents, they do not, by any means, speak with a united voice; in fact, many such parents actively support the call for adoption reform. Yet some adoptive parents genuinely fear what might happen if their child should discover the identity of natural parents — they fear that a transfer of love and affection will result. My own investigations indicate that there is no evidence to support such anxiety.

As the abortion debate becomes more heated, the Pro Life movement has come out strongly for maintaining secrecy in adoption proceedings, arguing that more and more young women will opt for abortion unless strict secrecy remains an essential part of all adoptions. It is not my purpose to enter the abortion debate, but it appalls me to hear such people advocate the continuation of an unfair and dishonest system of adoption in Canada as an alleged means of reducing the number of abortions.

In Canada, at the time of writing, nine of the provinces and the Yukon have responded to demands for reform by establishing adoption reunion registries. This has been an important step in recognizing that many birth parents and their adopted children seek some form of reunion. But, as already pointed out, most registries are passive in nature. They accept applications from the adult adoptees and natural parents and, if both parties register, will then arrange for communication between them. If, however, either party fails to register, the matter just sits. No further help is available to the individual who started the inquiry. This was the situation I faced in the search for my daughter.

Imperfect as adoption registries are, those seeking reunion have welcomed them all the same. As a result, most registries are flooded with applications. In Ontario alone, there may have been as many as two hundred thousand adoptions during the last sixty years, and half of those adoptees are now adults. The Ontario registry has almost nine thousand adoptees on file and there is a backlog of over two thousand applicants waiting to register. With these numbers, it is easy to see how inadequate funding can cause discontent and frustration. Even so, the registry has brought about over nine hundred reunions.

Recent developments in medical science have lent support to the cause of adoption reform in Canada. Over the last twenty years there has been a massive growth of information and knowledge in the field of genetics — so massive, in fact, that medical geneticists are today senior members of the team of practitioners at any modern maternity hospital. More and more couples are seeking the advice and counselling of geneticists — they know that they carry the building blocks of their future children within them, and not all those blocks may be sound. The adopted have the same concerns, but to receive genetic advice they need specific details of their family background. Without such details, the counsellor is powerless. It is thus hardly surprising that most adopted women begin searching for their birth parents when they want to start their own families — they want their babies to be healthy and therefore want to be aware of any possible inherited illness or impairment that might develop in their children. I well recall my own daughter's reaction when I asked her what it was that finally motivated her to begin her search. She said it was when a doctor ask her to complete a medical questionnaire about her young son. She had answered many such questions concerning herself with the word "unknown." But this response was not good enough when it concerned the health of her newborn son.

Our adoption system is not the only one in the world, and many people argue that others are functioning much better than ours. Scotland, for instance, instituted an open-record policy in the 1920s, and all of Great Britain has since created similar systems. In Finland and Israel adult adoptees may obtain their original birth certificates. There is no evidence from any of these countries suggesting that open records have led to either fewer adoptions, an increase in the number of abortions or a host of dissatisfied and unhappy adoptive parents.

The first change required is a very basic one of attitude. We must come to terms with the fact that adopted children can never be anything but the offspring of their natural parents. By pretending that they are "for all purposes" the children of their adoptive parents, we make them ashamed of their origin and place a burden of guilt upon them should they ever seek to find out for themselves who they really are. Equally important, we must accept the principle that, wherever individual rights seem to conflict, the child's rights must be paramount. The child is the sole party in the adoption process with no say in his or her outcome — to put it quite plainly, the fears and worries of adults, be they those of natural or adoptive parents, dictate what happens to a very young baby. These fears should never prejudice the fundamental rights of the child.

All adoption files should be available for inspection at the adoptee's age of majority. The right to examine these records should be automatic for the child and both the adoptive and natural parents. Where warranted, other family members such as grandparents and siblings should also have access. While I accept the arguments of both my newly found daughter and the social workers who say it is in the child's best interest to maintain secrecy while growing up within the adoptive family, the courts should be given discretion to grant file access at any time.

If these changes were made to our laws, adopted children would likely be able to locate their natural parents. They could go on to communicate with them if they wished to do so. With the element of secrecy removed, such contact would not be unexpected. Likewise, natural parents could also examine the file and initiate contact with their children. Any awkwardness or embarrassment caused by such an event would be more than offset by the over-all benefit of an open system. We believe that children become adults at the age of majority. They can then decide about their own lives. We must accept that they are also capable of dealing with contact by their natural parents.

While children are growing up in their adoptive homes, there should be a regular and continuous flow of information between the natural parents and adoptive parents. Perhaps once a year, the adoptive parents should submit a report about the child's development and progress. The natural parents should also present a statement of their activities for each preceding year, and a lawyer or social worker could then see to the exchange of this information. In this way, ideally, adopted children would grow up understanding that their natural parents were real people sharing concern about their welfare.

It would be easy to rewrite the laws governing all future adoptions. What to do about the thousands of adoptions that have already taken place is a far more vexing question. I suggest that there must first be an open admission that our governments made a commitment to confidentiality a long time ago which, with the experience of hindsight, has proven to be a mistake. To correct that mistake we must be both forthright and compassionate. There must be a period for those concerned to adjust to a new reality. Perhaps governments should announce that all existing adoption files be open to scrutiny by the adults concerned in three years' time.

Some people will react to this suggestion with fear and foreboding. No one can estimate how many mothers have a deep secret of a child given up for adoption that they have never revealed to anyone — particularly their husbands. I would welcome public discussion on this point more than any other.

Adoption reunion registries already in existence should take on new responsibilities by dealing with adoption records as they become available for examination. Where requested, they should be the agency that provides counselling, since reunions between adopted children and their blood parents are not always smooth or easy. Many people require support and assistance during reunion; while they are relieved to know the truth about their origins, they must sometimes learn to live with broken dreams as well.

Growing pressure on our governments has thus far, been insufficient to generate action. Much must yet be done to focus attention on the legitimate demands for adoption reform. It remains for those at each corner of the adoption triangle to continue to voice their demands until the politicians act.

This story has been about adoption and how our society created an unnatural system, shrouded in secrecy. In this respect, I fear we are about to relive our mistakes by failing to address similar issues connected with the new methods of conception. There is virtually no regulation of this practice, other than the personal ethics of the particular gynecologist involved with each case. The donors, such as countless young medical students, have been guaranteed anonymity. Once again, secrecy surrounds a procedure which has direct bearing on a human life. I see no reason why we should not expect a host of young men and women, concieved in this fashion, to begin searching for their natural fathers and mothers. These children will have the same motivation to learn of their biological past as do the adopted. The only reason we have not heard from them already is that most are still too young. They have not, as yet, begun to search.

Meeting and getting to know my daughter, a young woman I did not even know existed for so many years, has brought me immense happiness. When I began my search I did not expect to become involved in the growing movement for adoption reform, but I did. Many members of organizations such as Parent Finders had themselves been searching for their children for decades when I met them yet, despite their own frustrations, willingly gave me their support, sympathy and suggestions. In telling my story I have attempted to express my thanks to them and to assist their cause.

Selected Bibliography

Arndt, Melissa "Severed Roots: The Sealed Adoption Records Controversy." *Northern Illinois University Law Review*, Volume 6 (Winter 1986) 103-127

Crook, Marion *The Face In The Mirror: Teenagers Talk About Adoption* Toronto: New Canada Publications, A Division of NC Press Ltd., 1986

Disclosure Of Adoption Information Report of the Special Commissioner, Ralph Garber, D.S.W., To The Hon. John Sweeney, Minister Of Community & Social Services, Government of Ontario, November, 1985

Ehrlich, Henry *A Time To Search* New York: Paddington Press, 1977

Feigelman, William & Arnold R. Silverman *Chosen Children: New Patterns of Adoption Relationships* New York: Praeger Publishers, 1983

Ferguson, Evelyn B. "The Real Cabbage Patch Kids: An Examination of the Canadian Private Adoption System." *Occasional Papers In Social Policy, No. 2, Ontario Institute For Studies in Education* Toronto, (1984)

Harrington, Joseph D. "Adoption And The State Legislatures 1984-1985." *Public Welfare* (Spring 1986) 18-25
This publication is updated annually and may be obtained through The American Adoption Congress, PO Box 44040, L'Enfant Plaza Station, Washington, DC 20026-0040. This same organization will provide specific details as to each state's adoption disclosure laws and procedures.

Hepworth, H. Philip *Foster Care And Adoption In Canada* Ottawa: The Canadian Council on Social Development, 1980

Kirk, H. David *Adoption Kinship: A Modern Institution In Need Of Reform* Toronto: Butterworth & Co. (Canada) Ltd., 1981

Kirk, H. David *Shared Fate: A Theory & Method of Adoptive Relationships* (2nd Edition) Brentwood Bay, BC: Ben Simon Publications, 1984

Klibanoff, Susan & Elton *Let's Talk About Adoption* Boston & Toronto: Little Brown & Co., 1973

Lifton, Betty Jean *Lost & Found: The Adoption Experience* New York: Dial Press, 1983

Marcus, Clare *Adopted?: A Canadian Guide For Adopted Adults In Search Of Their Origins* North Vancouver: International Self Counsel Press Ltd., 1979

Marcus, Clare *Who Is My Mother?: Birth Parents, Adoptive Parents And Adoptees Talk About Living With Adoption And The Search For Lost Family* Toronto: Macmillan of Canada, 1981

Omenn, Gilbert S., Judith G. Hall and Kenneth D. Hansen "Genetic Counseling For Adoptees At Risk For Specific Inherited Disorders." *American Journal of Medical Genetics* 5 (1980) 157-164

Redmond, Wendis & Sherry Sleightholm *Once Removed: Voices From Inside The Adoption Triangle* Toronto: McGraw, Hill, Ryerson Ltd., 1986

Report: Committee On Record Disclosure To Adoptees A Report To The Hon. James A. Taylor, Q.C., Minister of

Community & Social Services, Government of Ontario, June 22, 1976

Rucker, Cynthia A. "Texas Adoption Laws And Adoptees' Rights Of Access To Confidential Records." St. *Mary's Law Journal*, Volume 15 (1983) 153-183

Sachdev, Paul (Editor) *Adoption: Current Issues & Trends* Toronto: Butterworths, 1984

Sachdev, Paul *Unlocking The Adoption Files* Memorial University, Newfoundland, 1988

Sorosky, Arthur D., Annette Baran, Reuben Pannor *The Adoption Triangle: The Effects Of The Sealed Record On Adoptees, Birth Parents & Adoptive Parents* Garden City, New York: Anchor Press, 1978

Tartanella, Paul J. "Sealed Adoption Records And The Consititutional Right Of Privacy Of The Natural Parent." *Rutgers Law Review*, Volume 34 (Spring 1982) 451-490

Triseliotis, John *In Search Of Origins: The Experience of Adopted People* London & Boston: Routledge & Kegan Paul, 1973

Weaver, David D. & Luis F. Escobar "Letter To The Editor: Twenty-Four Ways To Have Children." *American Journal of Medical Genetics* 26 (1987) 737-740

In Canada, every provincial ministry responsible for child welfare and adoption publishes an annual report which contains statistics as to the number of adoptions, age and ethnic background, etc. The adoption reunion registries in each province also produce annual reports on the number of registrations and reunions processed each year by the agency. Each registry has its own regulations and procedures which seem to change frequently. Most make available pamphlets outlining the work of the registry. All these publications can be obtained from the relevant government office in each province.

The provincial chapters of Parent Finders and the Canadian Adoptees Reform Association publish various pamphlets and newsletters which are available through their offices. I was particularly impressed with the background information and material maintained by TRIAD (Society For Truth In Adoption), Box 5114, Station A, Calgary, Alberta, Canada, T2H 1X1.